33728

The Boston Tea Party

MILL STREET ELEMENTARY SCHOOL

written and illustrated by
Rod Espinosa

magic
wagon

visit us at
www.abdopublishing.com

Published by Magic Wagon, a division of the ABDO Publishing Group, 8000 West 78th Street, Edina, Minnesota 55439. Copyright © 2008 by Abdo Consulting Group, Inc. International copyrights reserved in all countries. All rights reserved. No part of this book may be reproduced in any form without written permission from the publisher. Graphic Planet™ is a trademark and logo of Magic Wagon.

Printed in the United States.

Written and Illustrated by Rod Espinosa
Colored and Lettered by Rod Espinosa
Edited by Stephanie Hedlund
Interior layout and design by Antarctic Press
Cover art by Rod Espinosa
Cover design by Neil Klinepier

Library of Congress Cataloging-in-Publication Data

Espinosa, Rod.
    The Boston Tea Party / written and illustrated by Rod Espinosa.
    p. cm. -- (Graphic history)
    Includes index.
    ISBN 978-1-60270-075-8
    1. Boston Tea Party, 1773--Juvenile literature. 2. Graphic novels. I. Title.
E215.7.E77 2008
973.3'115--dc22

                                2007006440

TABLE of CONTENTS

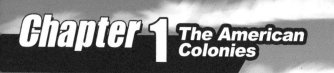

Chapter 1 The American Colonies

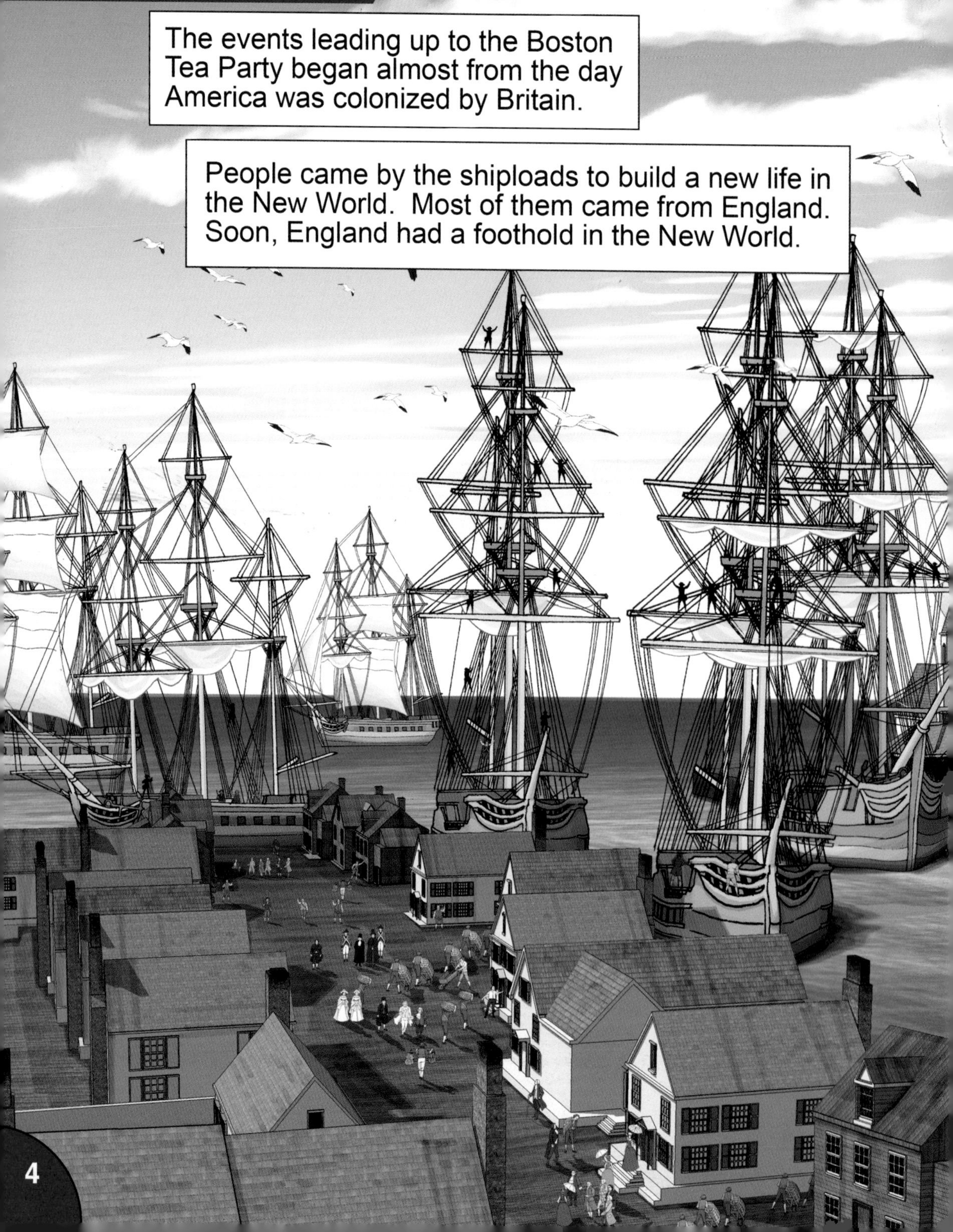

The events leading up to the Boston Tea Party began almost from the day America was colonized by Britain.
People came by the shiploads to build a new life in the New World. Most of them came from England. Soon, England had a foothold in the New World.

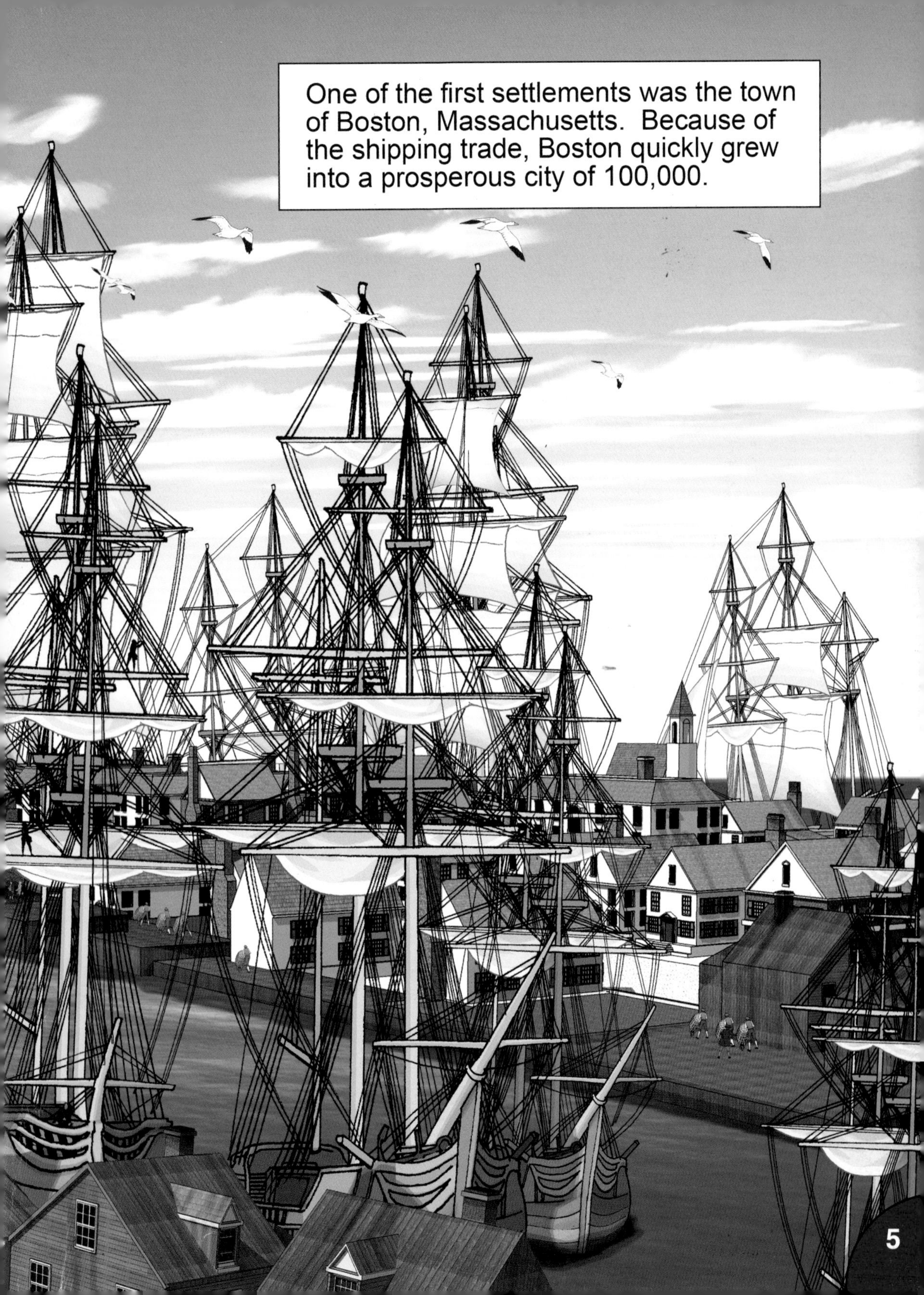
One of the first settlements was the town of Boston, Massachusetts. Because of the shipping trade, Boston quickly grew into a prosperous city of 100,000.

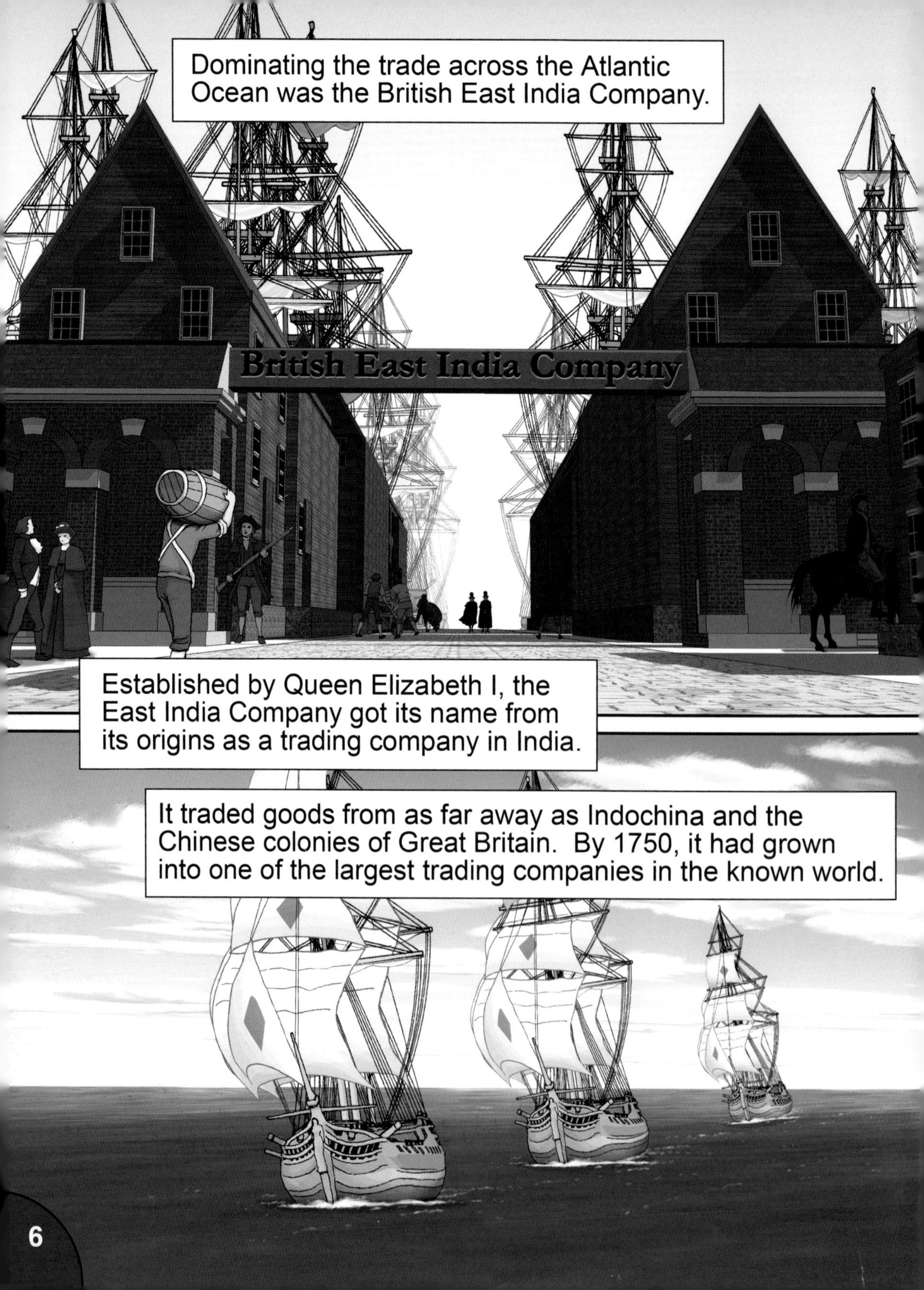
Dominating the trade across the Atlantic Ocean was the British East India Company.
British East India Company
Established by Queen Elizabeth I, the East India Company got its name from its origins as a trading company in India.
It traded goods from as far away as Indochina and the Chinese colonies of Great Britain. By 1750, it had grown into one of the largest trading companies in the known world.

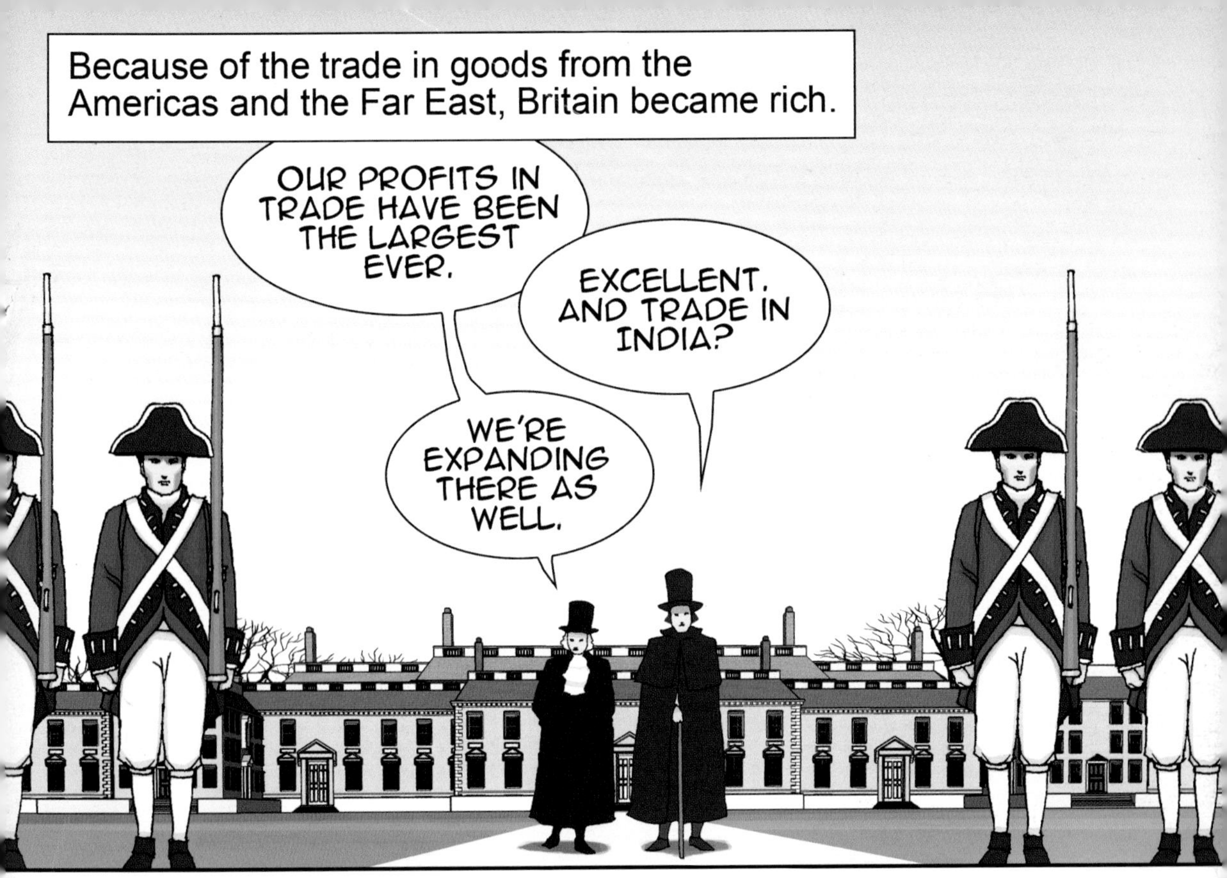
Because of the trade in goods from the Americas and the Far East, Britain became rich.
OUR PROFITS IN TRADE HAVE BEEN THE LARGEST EVER.
EXCELLENT. AND TRADE IN INDIA?
WE'RE EXPANDING THERE AS WELL.

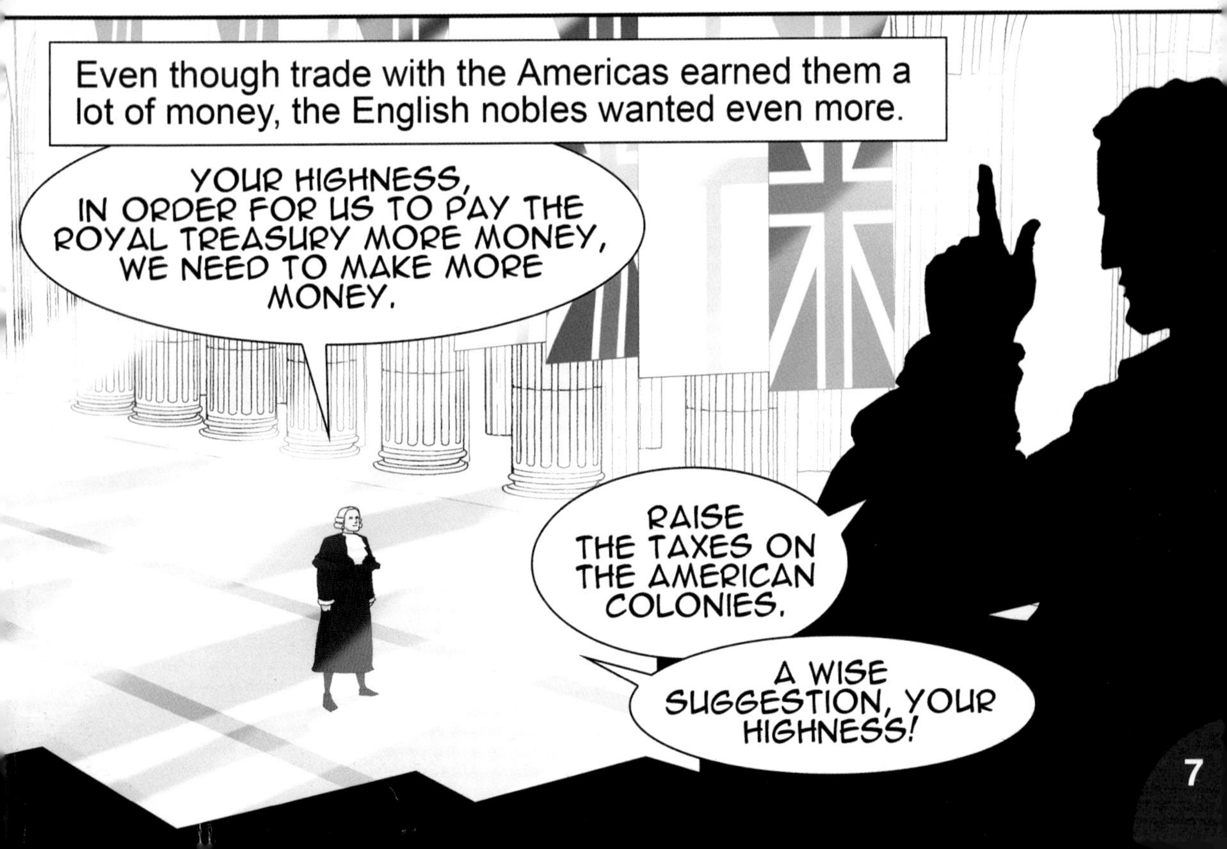
Even though trade with the Americas earned them a lot of money, the English nobles wanted even more.
YOUR HIGHNESS, IN ORDER FOR US TO PAY THE ROYAL TREASURY MORE MONEY, WE NEED TO MAKE MORE MONEY.
RAISE THE TAXES ON THE AMERICAN COLONIES.
A WISE SUGGESTION, YOUR HIGHNESS!

The new settlers were not all Englishmen. There were immigrants from other countries too. They all came to America to start a new life, not to be ruled by the British Empire.

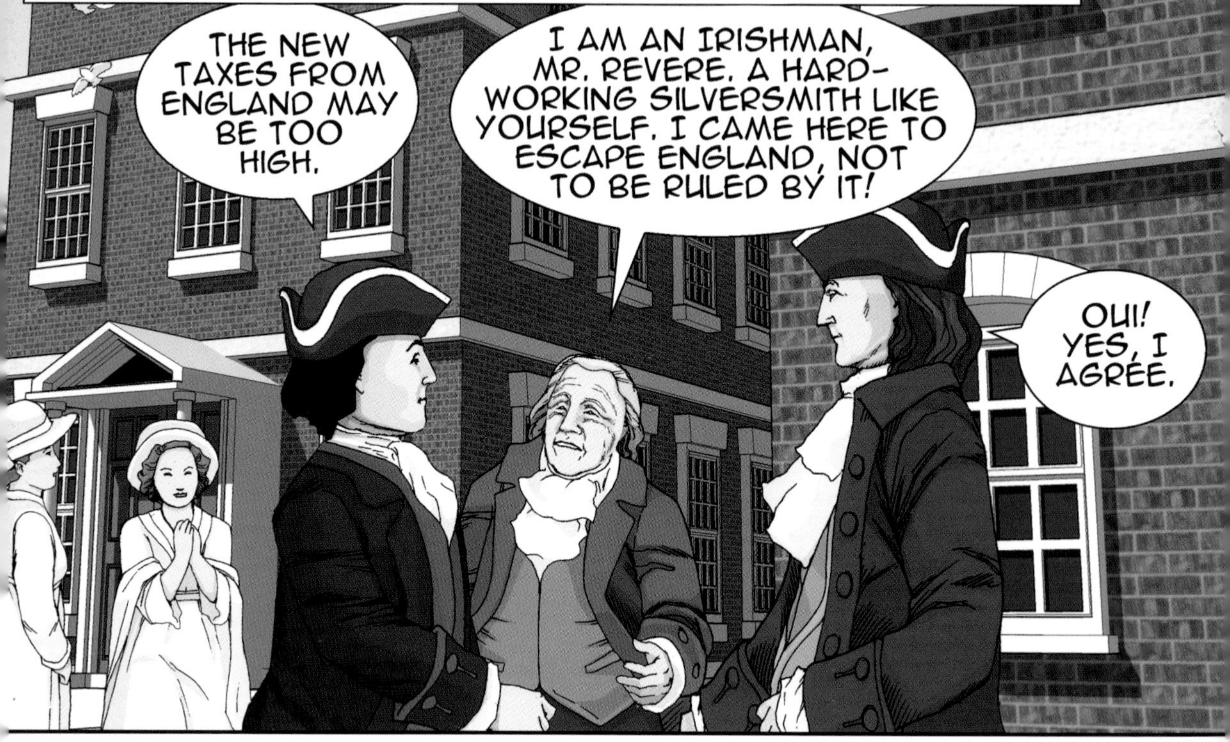

THE NEW TAXES FROM ENGLAND MAY BE TOO HIGH.
I AM AN IRISHMAN, MR. REVERE. A HARD-WORKING SILVERSMITH LIKE YOURSELF. I CAME HERE TO ESCAPE ENGLAND, NOT TO BE RULED BY IT!
OUI! YES, I AGREE.

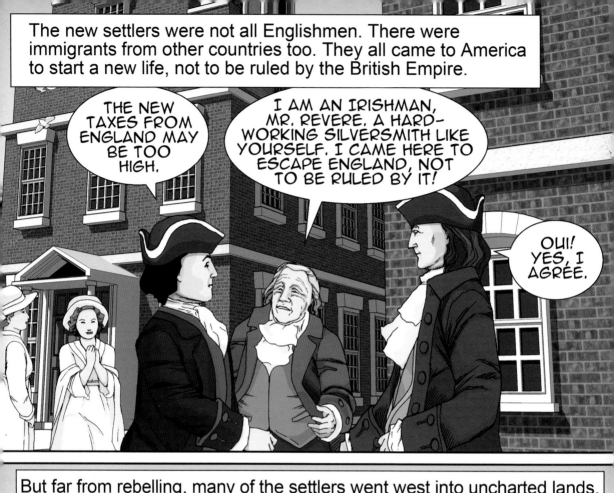

But far from rebelling, many of the settlers went west into uncharted lands.

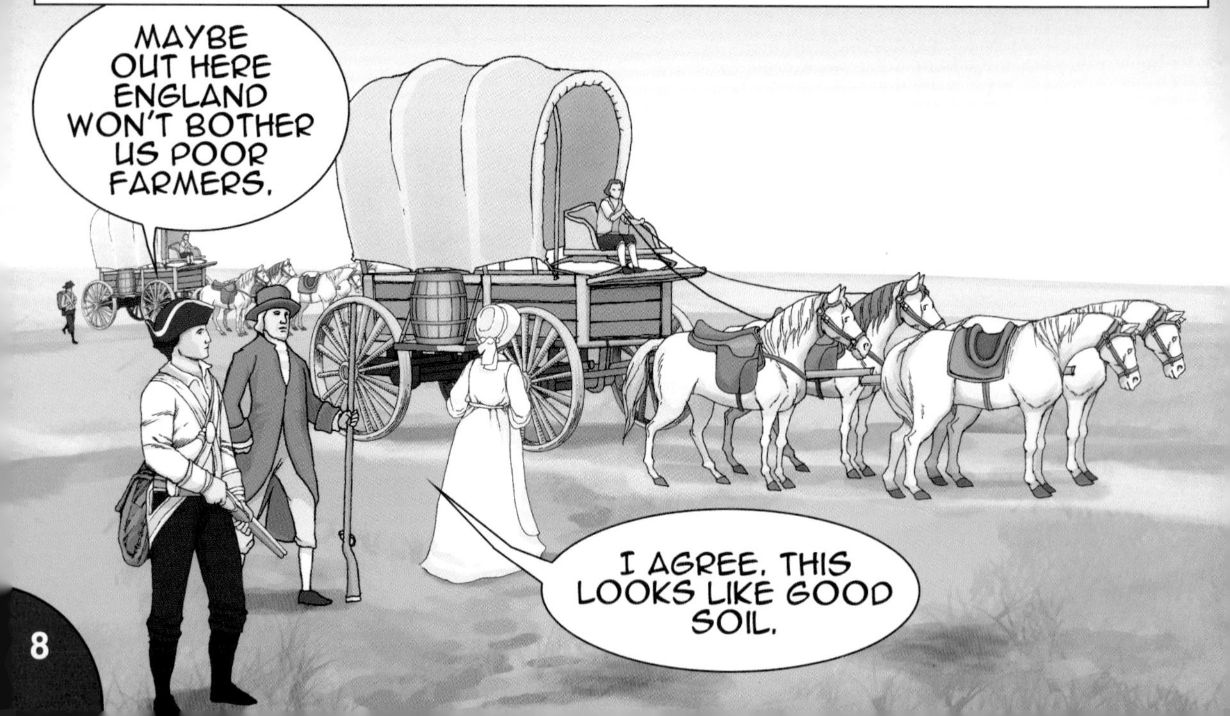

MAYBE OUT HERE ENGLAND WON'T BOTHER US POOR FARMERS.
I AGREE. THIS LOOKS LIKE GOOD SOIL.

Chapter 2 The French and Indian War

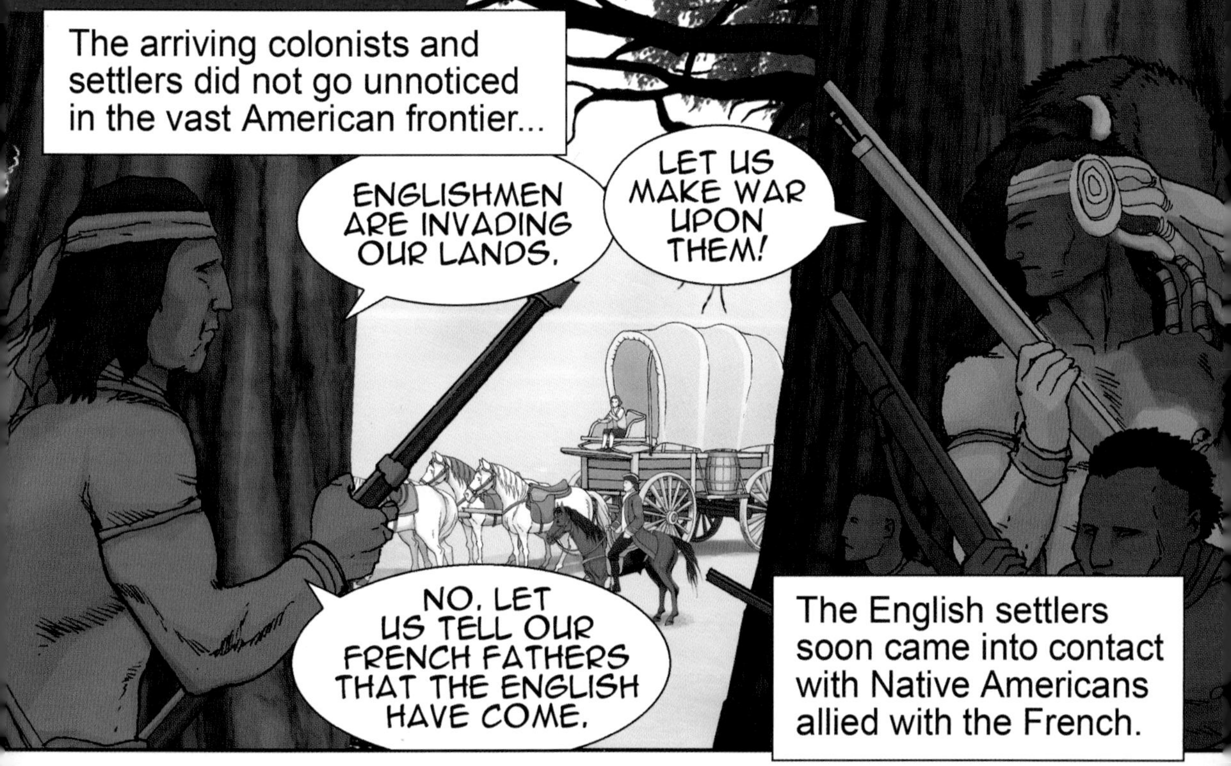
The arriving colonists and settlers did not go unnoticed in the vast American frontier...
ENGLISHMEN ARE INVADING OUR LANDS.
LET US MAKE WAR UPON THEM!
NO. LET US TELL OUR FRENCH FATHERS THAT THE ENGLISH HAVE COME.
The English settlers soon came into contact with Native Americans allied with the French.

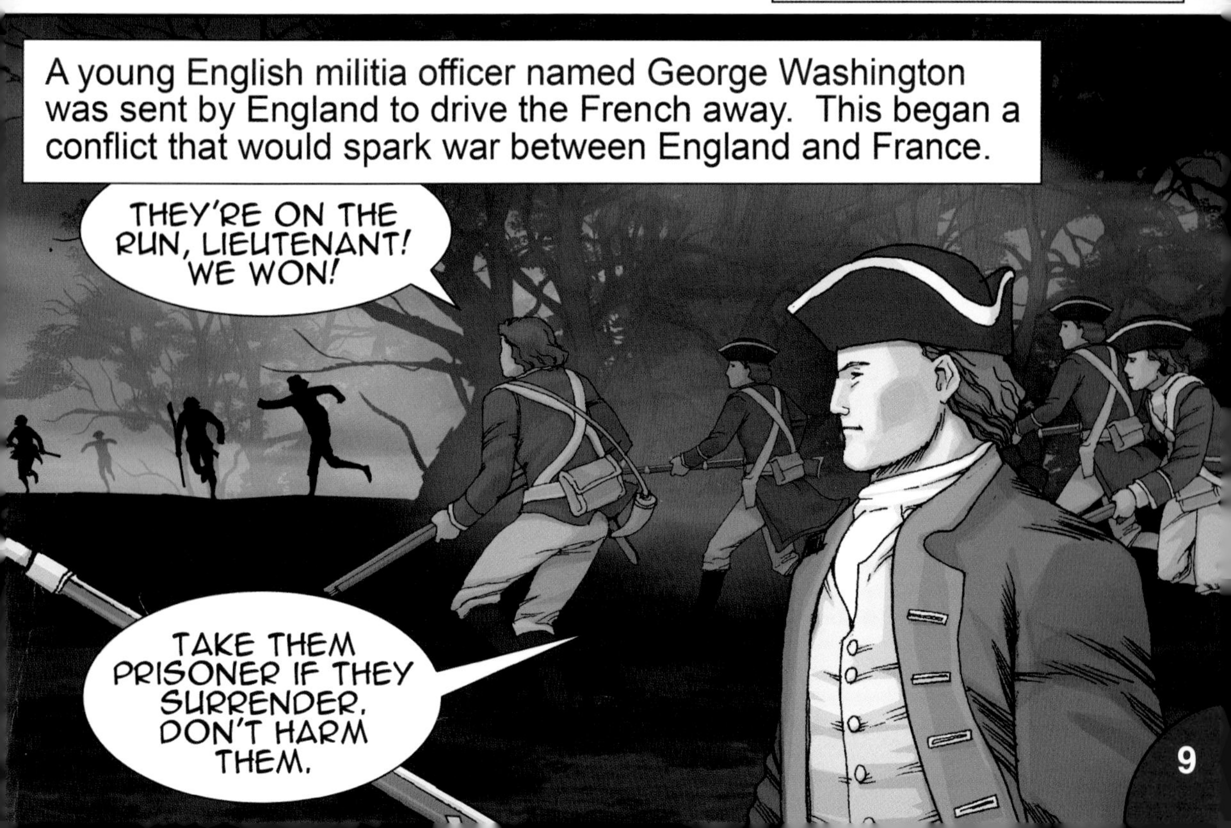
A young English militia officer named George Washington was sent by England to drive the French away. This began a conflict that would spark war between England and France.
THEY'RE ON THE RUN, LIEUTENANT! WE WON!
TAKE THEM PRISONER IF THEY SURRENDER. DON'T HARM THEM.

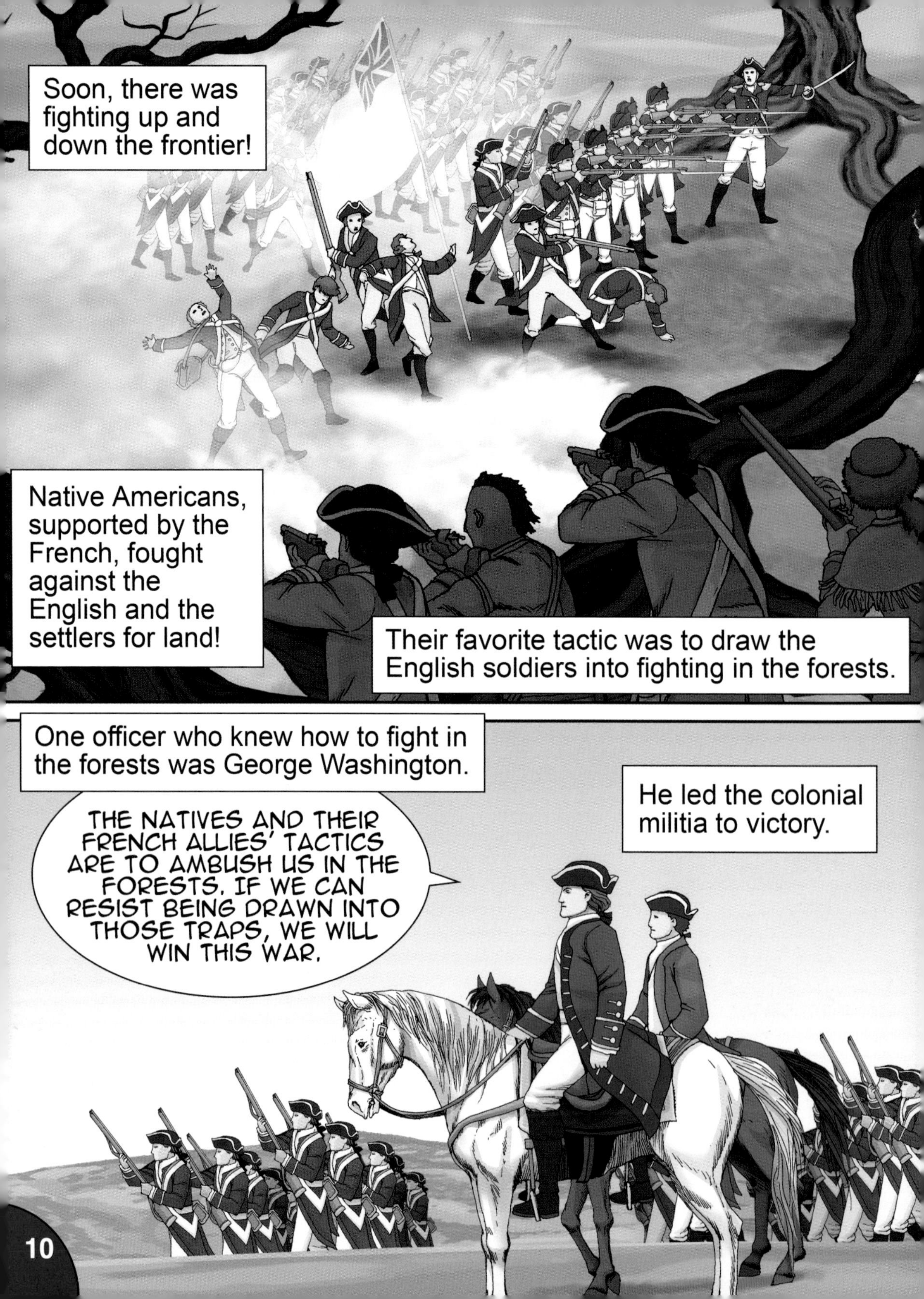
Soon, there was fighting up and down the frontier!
Native Americans, supported by the French, fought against the English and the settlers for land!
Their favorite tactic was to draw the English soldiers into fighting in the forests.
One officer who knew how to fight in the forests was George Washington.
THE NATIVES AND THEIR FRENCH ALLIES' TACTICS ARE TO AMBUSH US IN THE FORESTS. IF WE CAN RESIST BEING DRAWN INTO THOSE TRAPS, WE WILL WIN THIS WAR.
He led the colonial militia to victory.

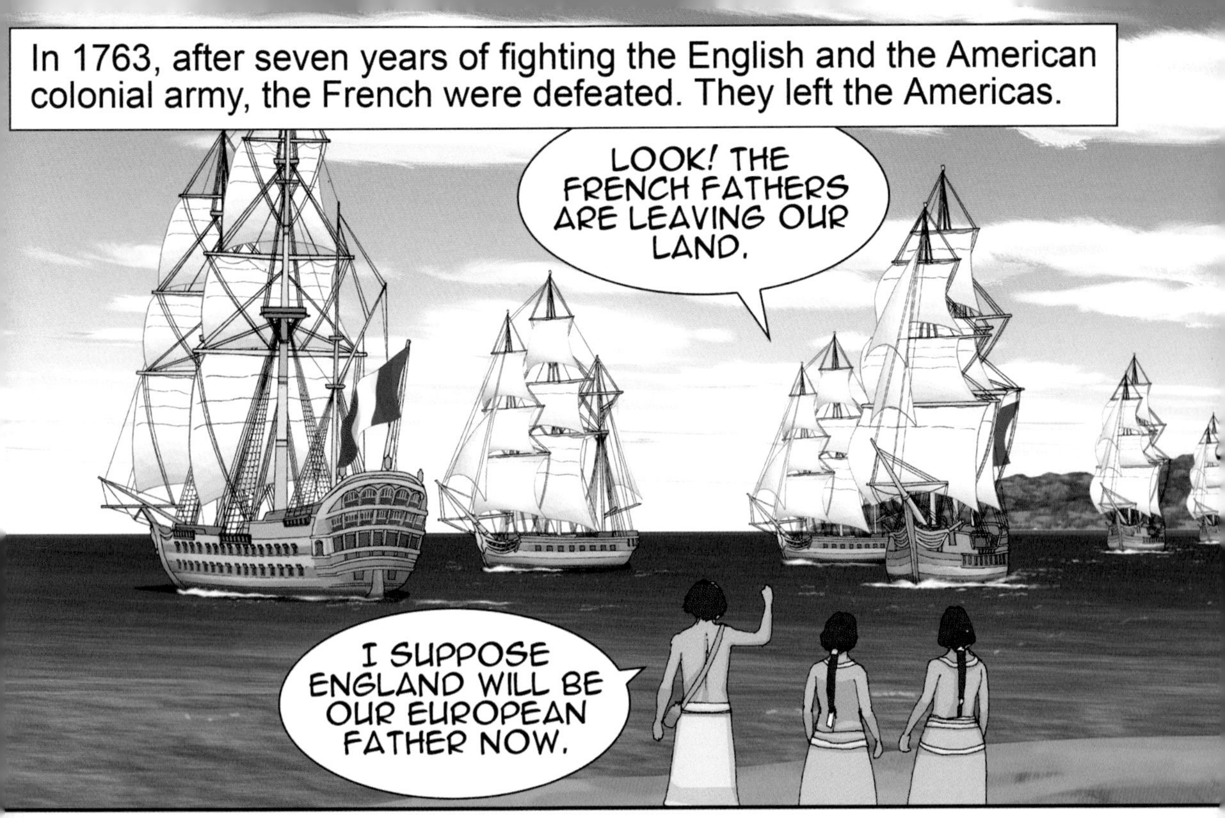
In 1763, after seven years of fighting the English and the American colonial army, the French were defeated. They left the Americas.
LOOK! THE FRENCH FATHERS ARE LEAVING OUR LAND.
I SUPPOSE ENGLAND WILL BE OUR EUROPEAN FATHER NOW.

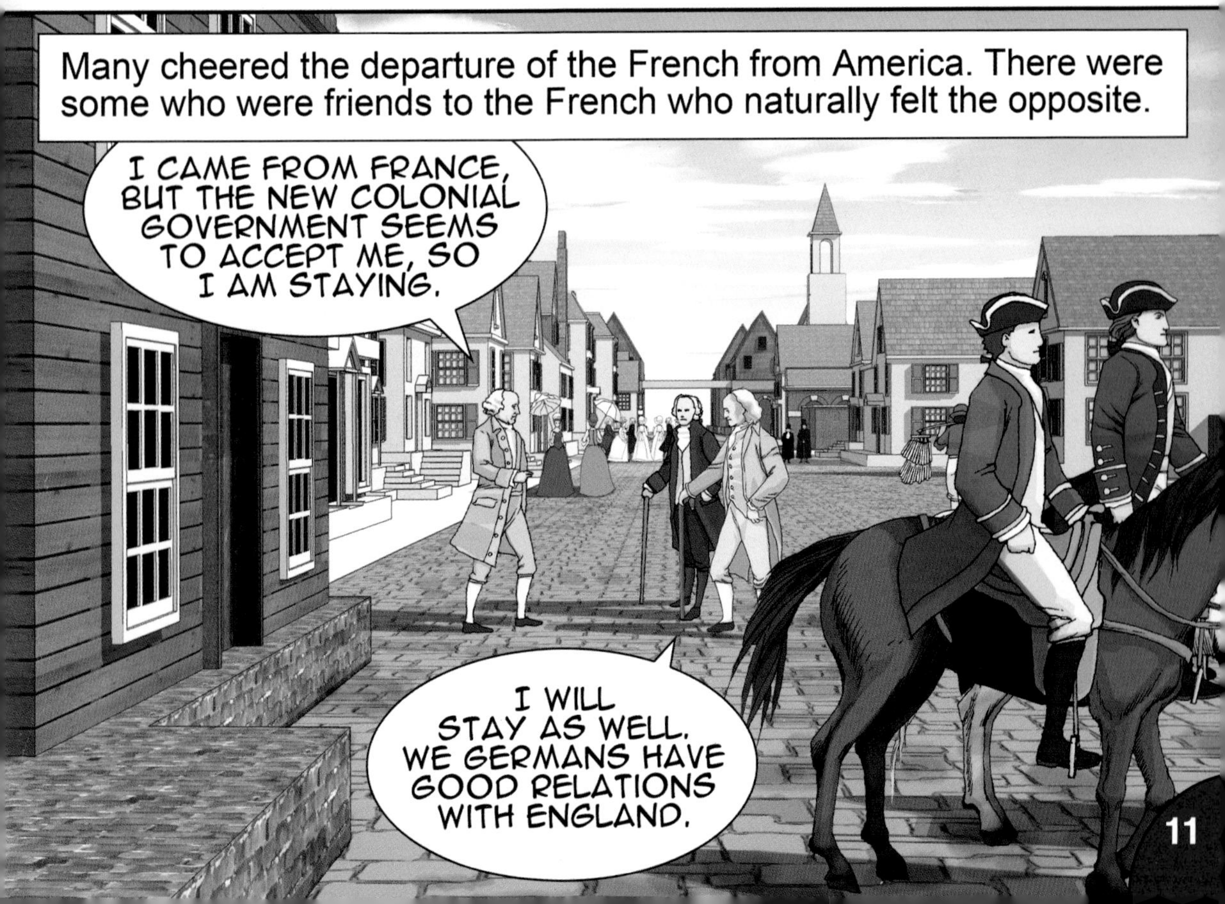
Many cheered the departure of the French from America. There were some who were friends to the French who naturally felt the opposite.
I CAME FROM FRANCE, BUT THE NEW COLONIAL GOVERNMENT SEEMS TO ACCEPT ME, SO I AM STAYING.
I WILL STAY AS WELL. WE GERMANS HAVE GOOD RELATIONS WITH ENGLAND.

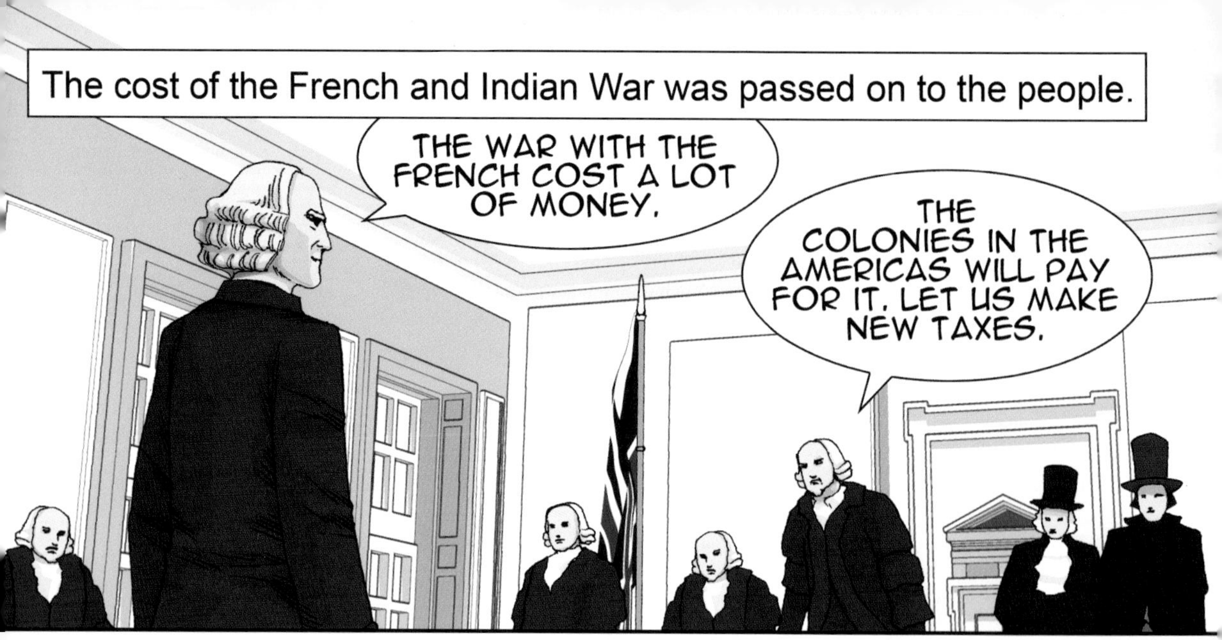
The cost of the French and Indian War was passed on to the people.
THE WAR WITH THE FRENCH COST A LOT OF MONEY.
THE COLONIES IN THE AMERICAS WILL PAY FOR IT. LET US MAKE NEW TAXES.

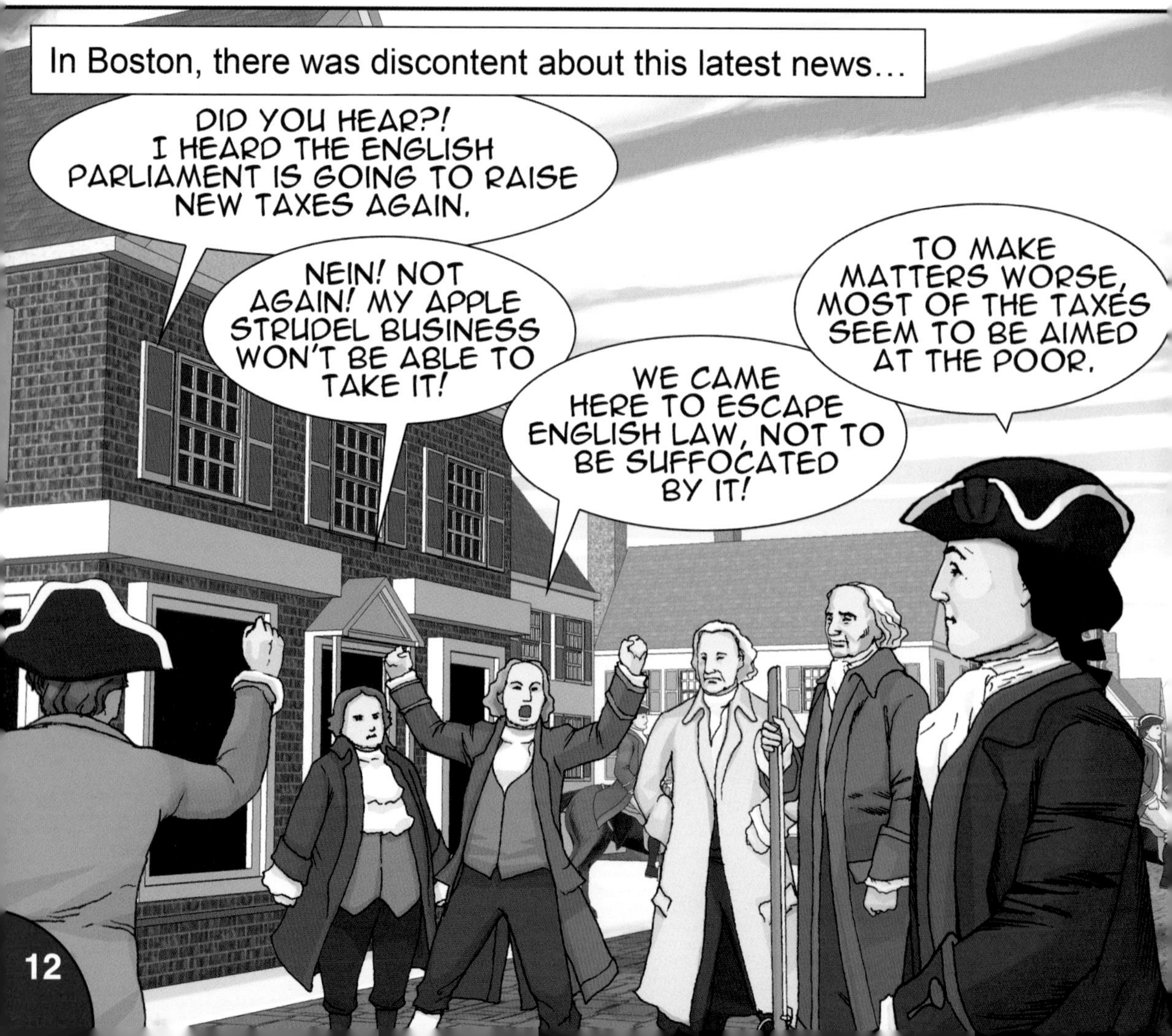
In Boston, there was discontent about this latest news…
DID YOU HEAR?! I HEARD THE ENGLISH PARLIAMENT IS GOING TO RAISE NEW TAXES AGAIN.
NEIN! NOT AGAIN! MY APPLE STRUDEL BUSINESS WON'T BE ABLE TO TAKE IT!
WE CAME HERE TO ESCAPE ENGLISH LAW, NOT TO BE SUFFOCATED BY IT!
TO MAKE MATTERS WORSE, MOST OF THE TAXES SEEM TO BE AIMED AT THE POOR.

Chapter 3 The Stamp Act

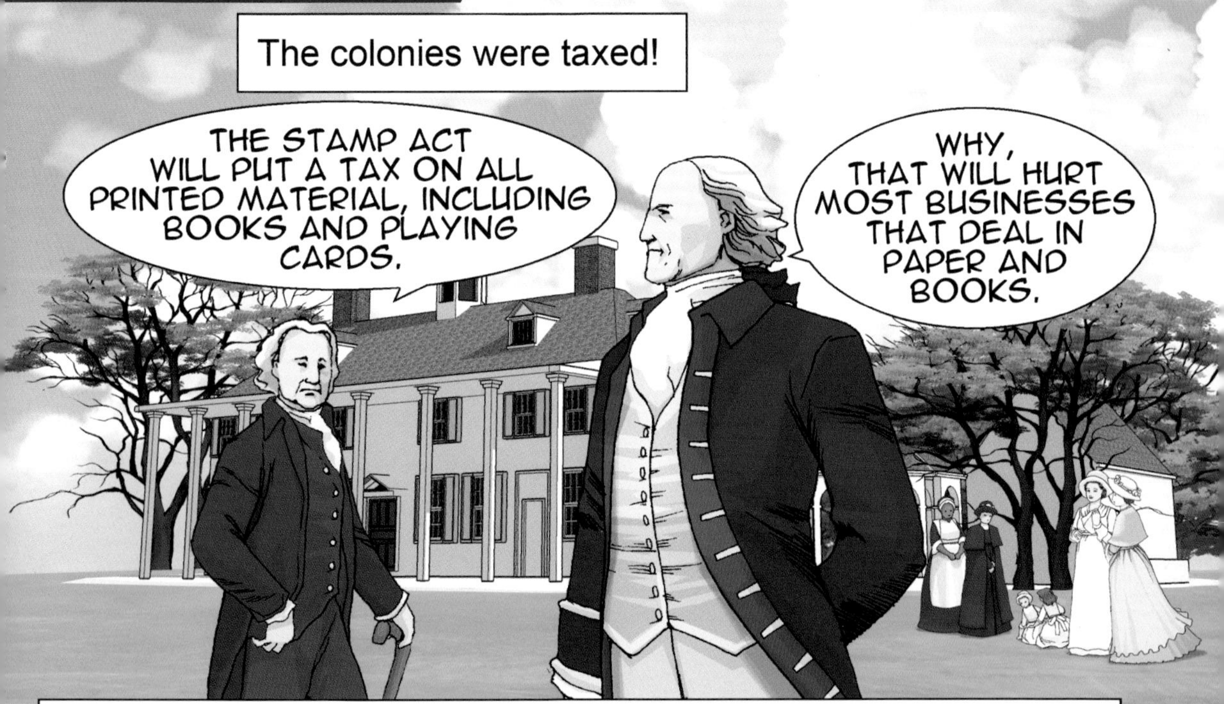
The colonies were taxed!
THE STAMP ACT WILL PUT A TAX ON ALL PRINTED MATERIAL, INCLUDING BOOKS AND PLAYING CARDS.
WHY, THAT WILL HURT MOST BUSINESSES THAT DEAL IN PAPER AND BOOKS.

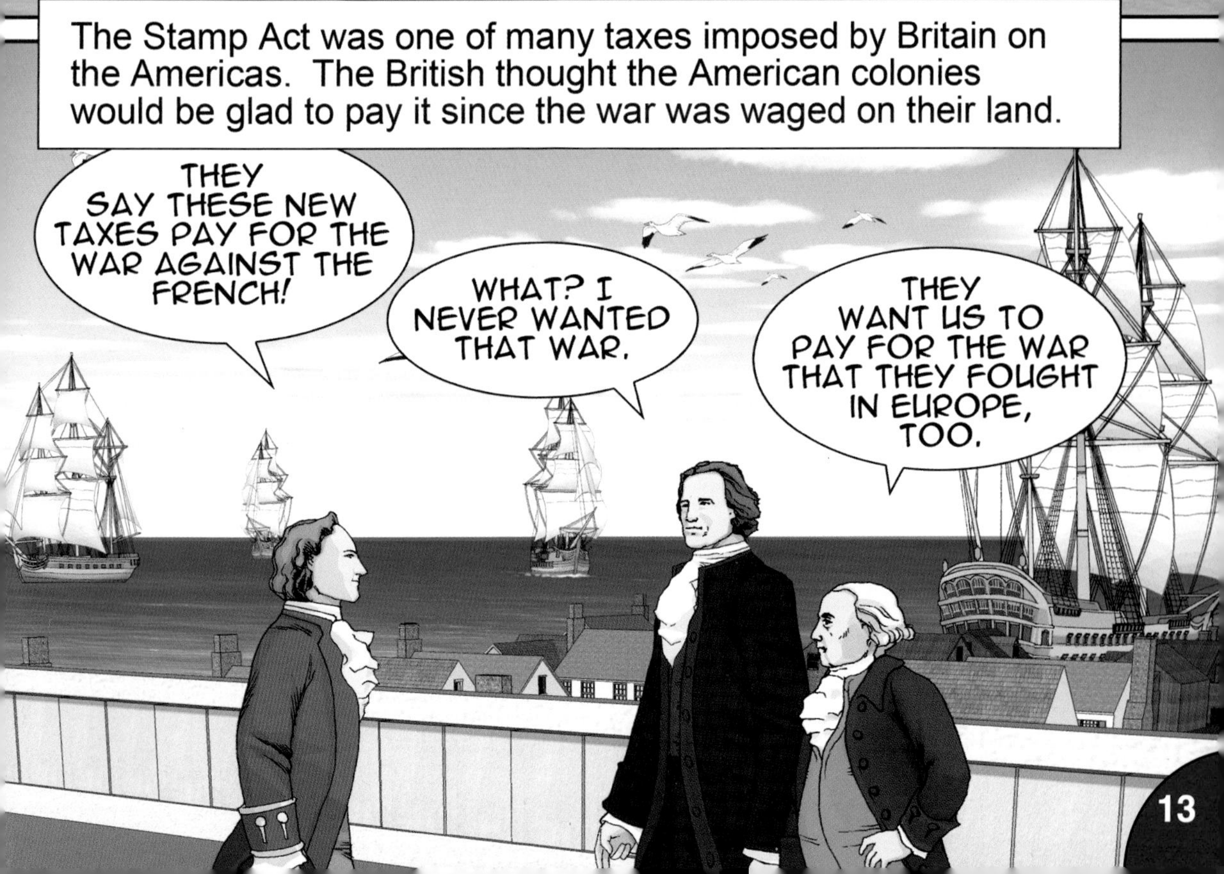
The Stamp Act was one of many taxes imposed by Britain on the Americas. The British thought the American colonies would be glad to pay it since the war was waged on their land.
THEY SAY THESE NEW TAXES PAY FOR THE WAR AGAINST THE FRENCH!
WHAT? I NEVER WANTED THAT WAR.
THEY WANT US TO PAY FOR THE WAR THAT THEY FOUGHT IN EUROPE, TOO.

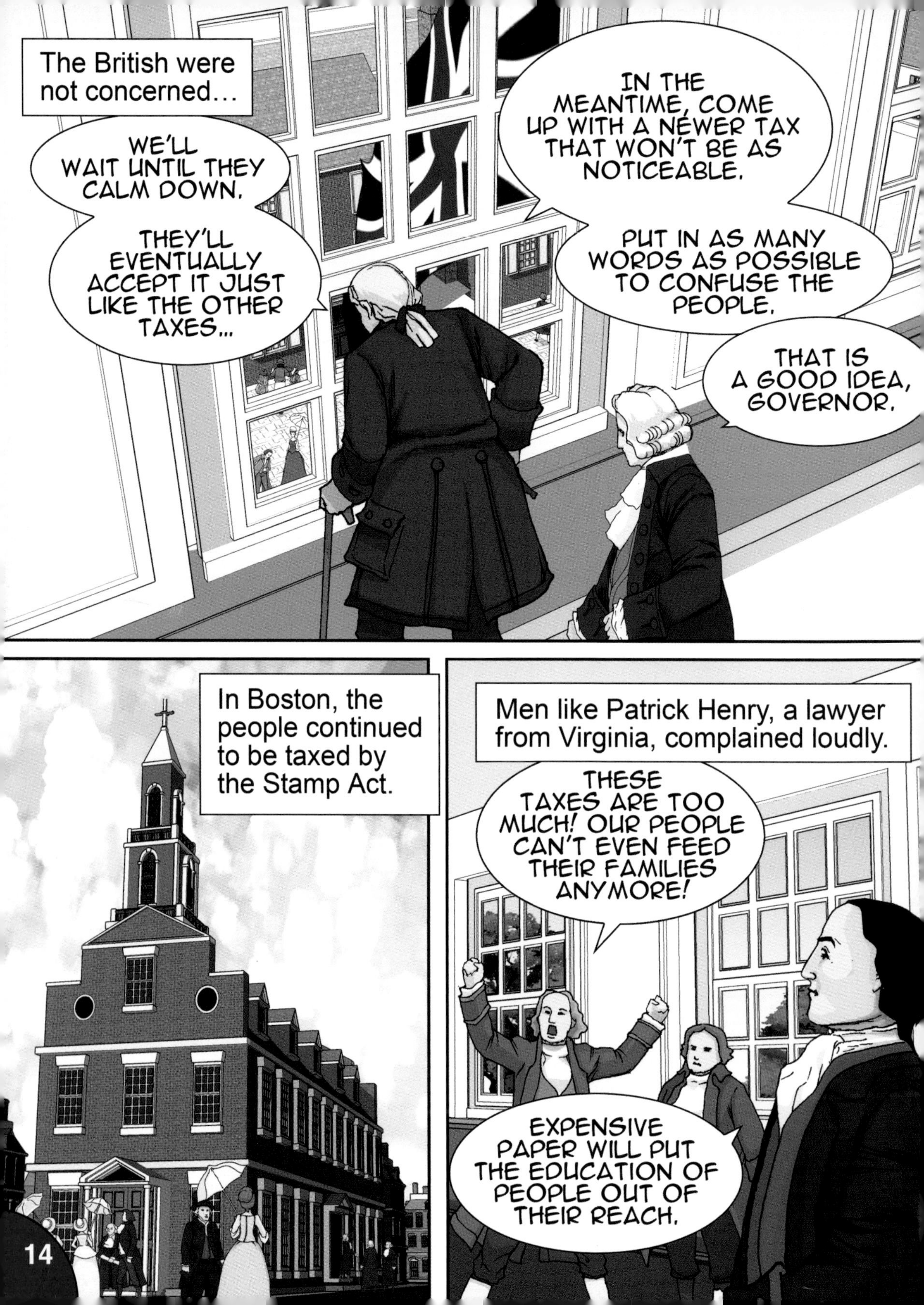
The British were not concerned…
WE'LL WAIT UNTIL THEY CALM DOWN.
THEY'LL EVENTUALLY ACCEPT IT JUST LIKE THE OTHER TAXES...
IN THE MEANTIME, COME UP WITH A NEWER TAX THAT WON'T BE AS NOTICEABLE.
PUT IN AS MANY WORDS AS POSSIBLE TO CONFUSE THE PEOPLE.
THAT IS A GOOD IDEA, GOVERNOR.
In Boston, the people continued to be taxed by the Stamp Act.
Men like Patrick Henry, a lawyer from Virginia, complained loudly.
THESE TAXES ARE TOO MUCH! OUR PEOPLE CAN'T EVEN FEED THEIR FAMILIES ANYMORE!
EXPENSIVE PAPER WILL PUT THE EDUCATION OF PEOPLE OUT OF THEIR REACH.

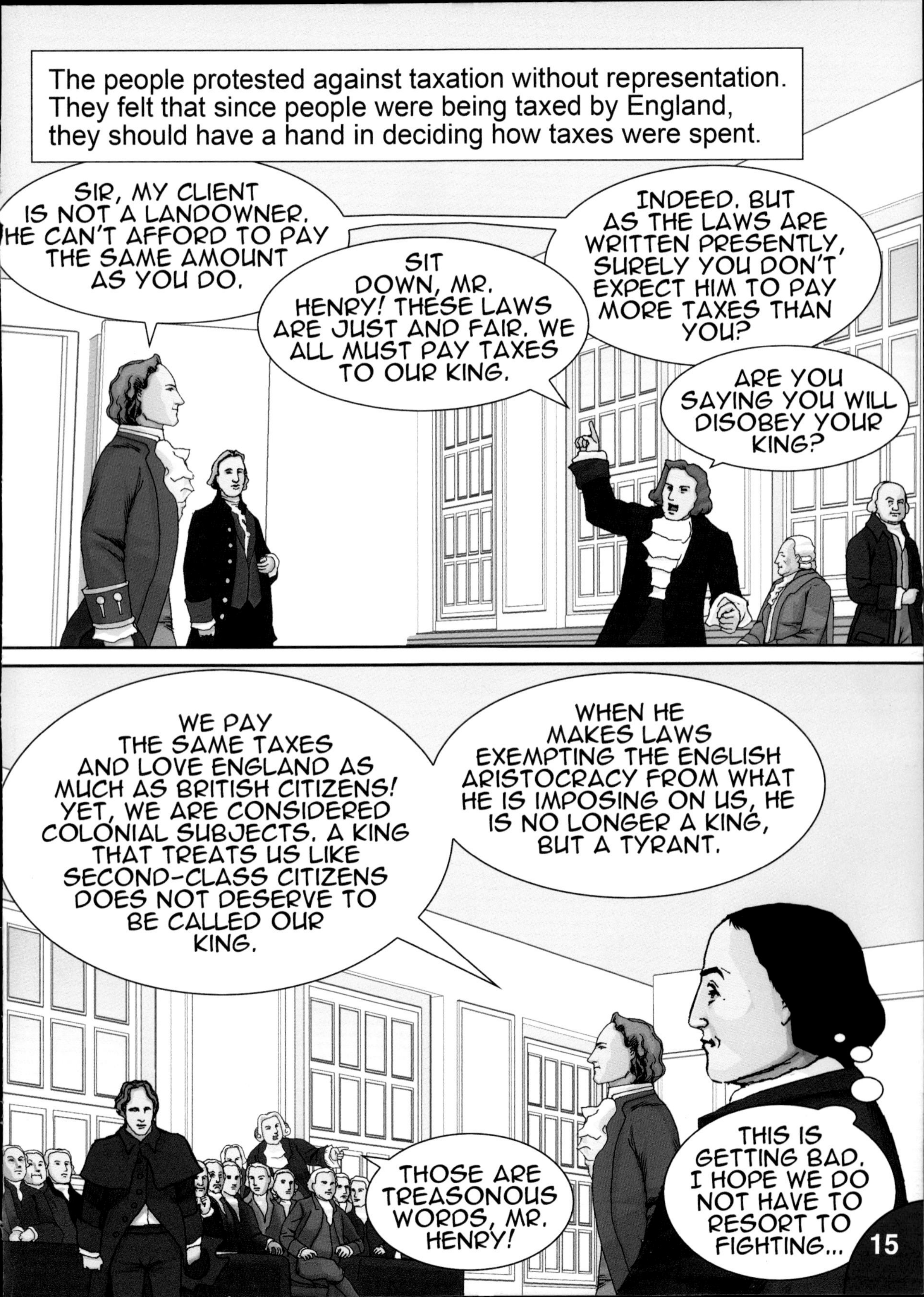
The people protested against taxation without representation. They felt that since people were being taxed by England, they should have a hand in deciding how taxes were spent.
SIR, MY CLIENT IS NOT A LANDOWNER. HE CAN'T AFFORD TO PAY THE SAME AMOUNT AS YOU DO.
SIT DOWN, MR. HENRY! THESE LAWS ARE JUST AND FAIR. WE ALL MUST PAY TAXES TO OUR KING.
INDEED. BUT AS THE LAWS ARE WRITTEN PRESENTLY, SURELY YOU DON'T EXPECT HIM TO PAY MORE TAXES THAN YOU?
ARE YOU SAYING YOU WILL DISOBEY YOUR KING?
WE PAY THE SAME TAXES AND LOVE ENGLAND AS MUCH AS BRITISH CITIZENS! YET, WE ARE CONSIDERED COLONIAL SUBJECTS. A KING THAT TREATS US LIKE SECOND-CLASS CITIZENS DOES NOT DESERVE TO BE CALLED OUR KING.
WHEN HE MAKES LAWS EXEMPTING THE ENGLISH ARISTOCRACY FROM WHAT HE IS IMPOSING ON US, HE IS NO LONGER A KING, BUT A TYRANT.
THOSE ARE TREASONOUS WORDS, MR. HENRY!
THIS IS GETTING BAD. I HOPE WE DO NOT HAVE TO RESORT TO FIGHTING...

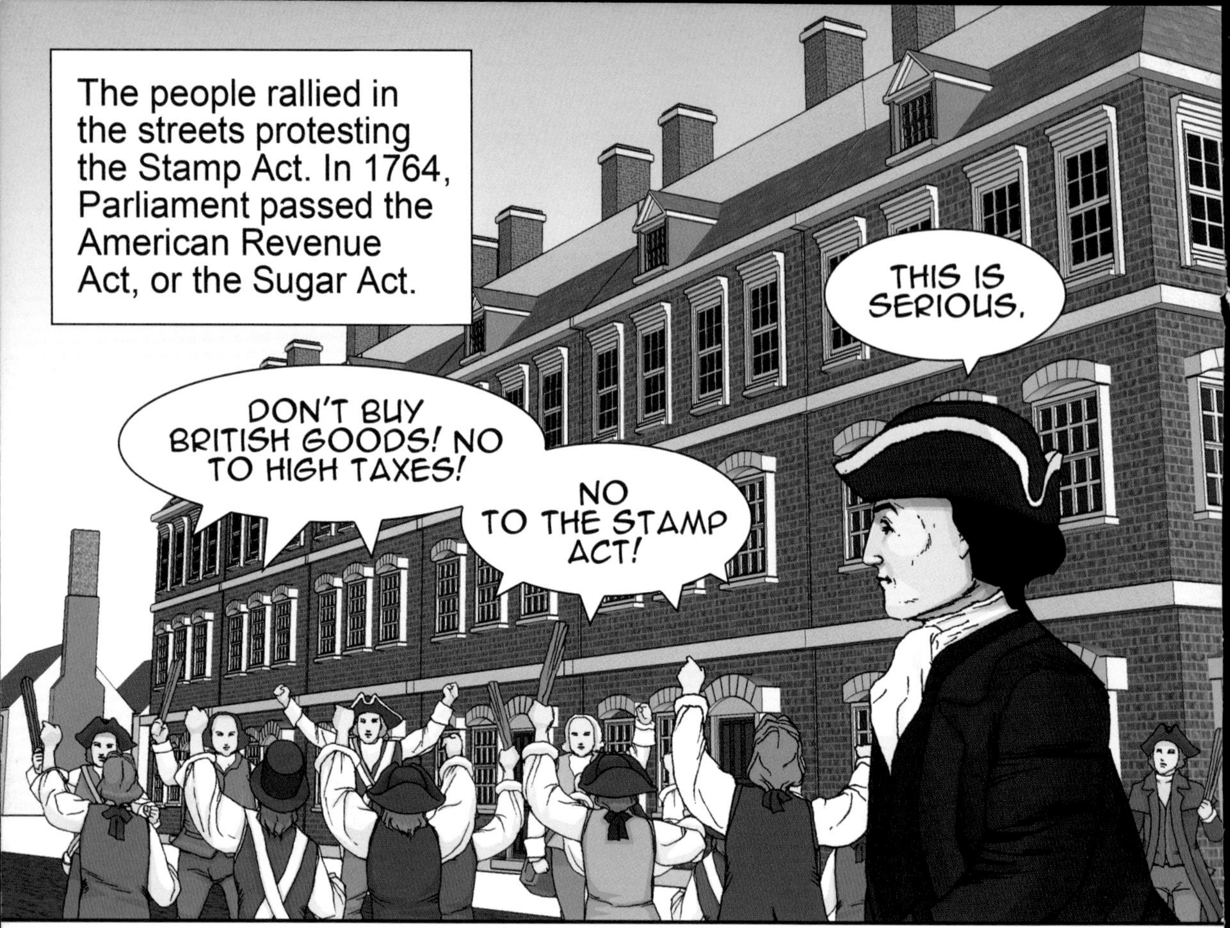
The people rallied in the streets protesting the Stamp Act. In 1764, Parliament passed the American Revenue Act, or the Sugar Act.
DON'T BUY BRITISH GOODS! NO TO HIGH TAXES!
NO TO THE STAMP ACT!
THIS IS SERIOUS.

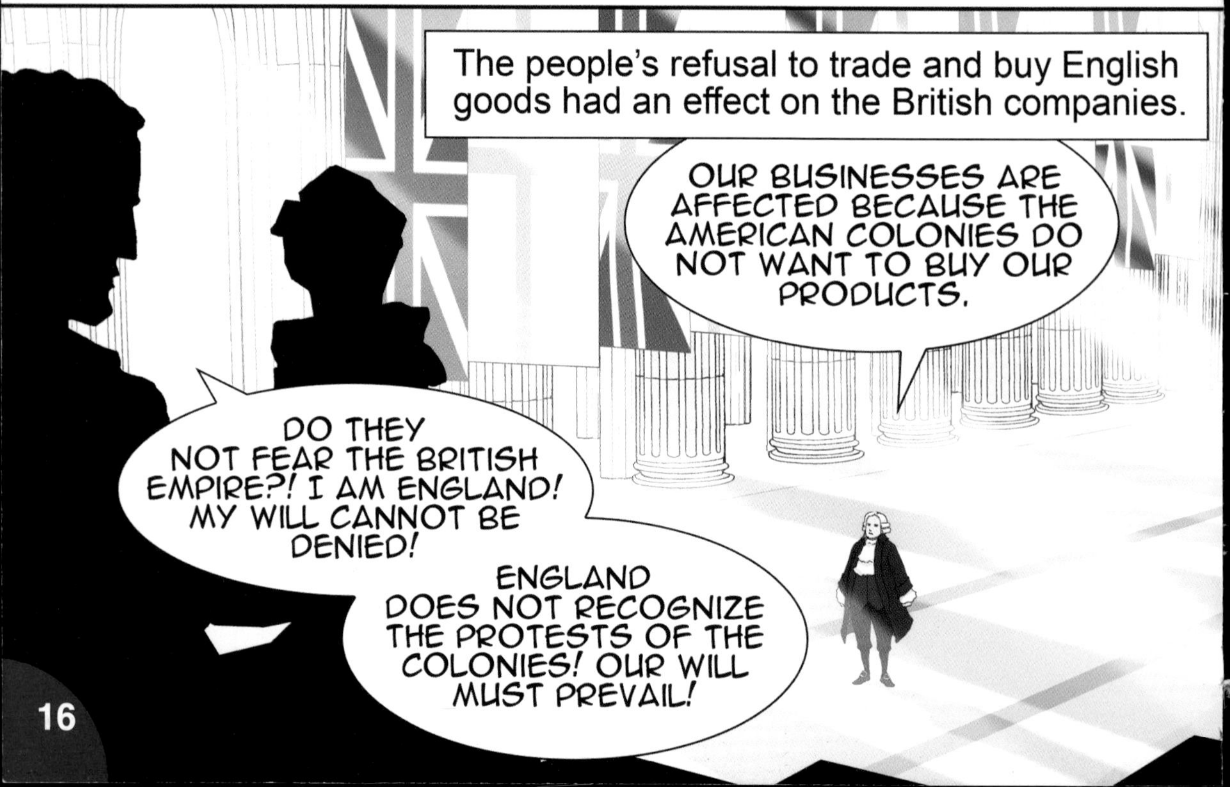
The people's refusal to trade and buy English goods had an effect on the British companies.
OUR BUSINESSES ARE AFFECTED BECAUSE THE AMERICAN COLONIES DO NOT WANT TO BUY OUR PRODUCTS.
DO THEY NOT FEAR THE BRITISH EMPIRE?! I AM ENGLAND! MY WILL CANNOT BE DENIED!
ENGLAND DOES NOT RECOGNIZE THE PROTESTS OF THE COLONIES! OUR WILL MUST PREVAIL!

Chapter 4 The Tea Tax

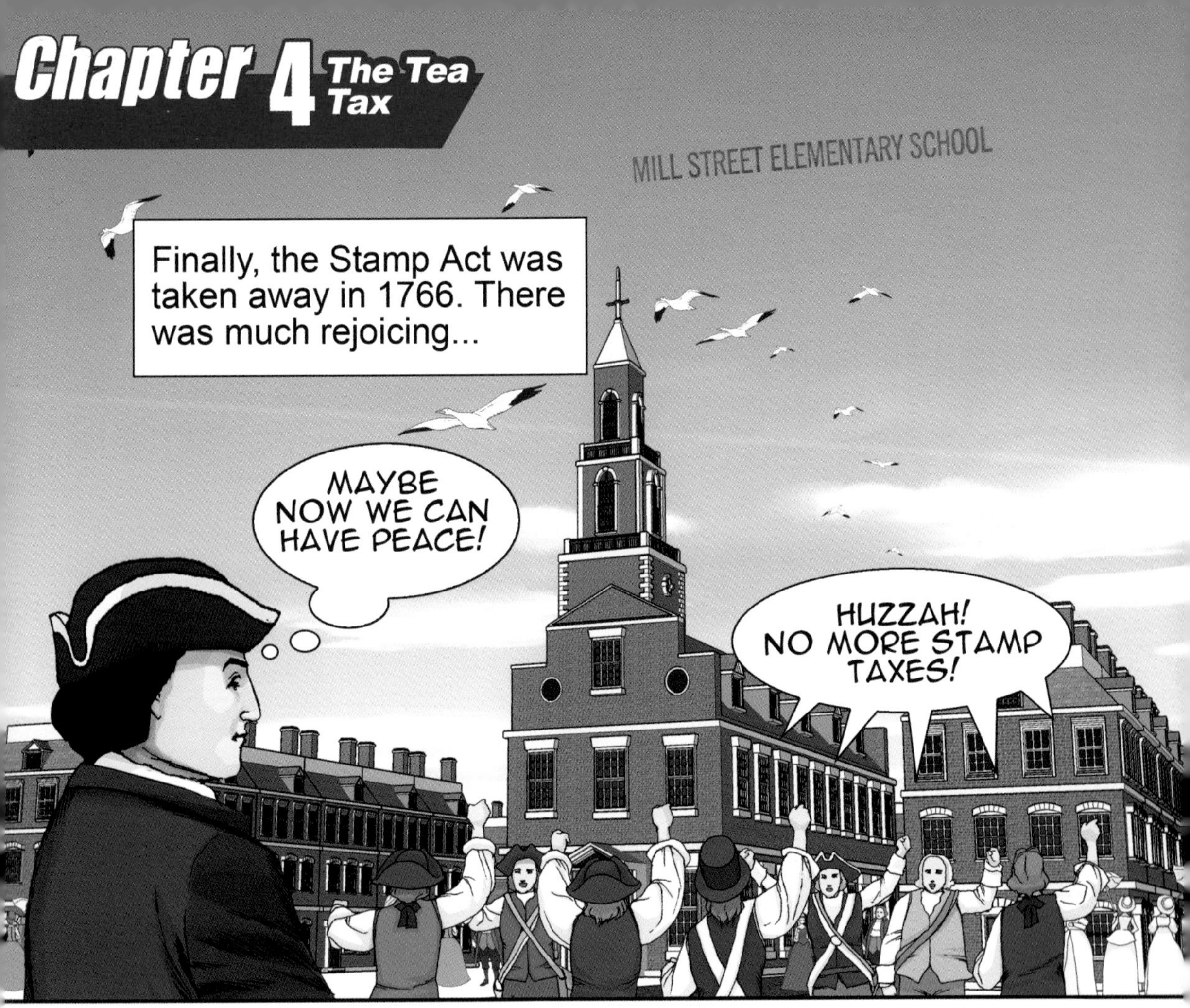
Finally, the Stamp Act was taken away in 1766. There was much rejoicing...
MAYBE NOW WE CAN HAVE PEACE!
HUZZAH! NO MORE STAMP TAXES!

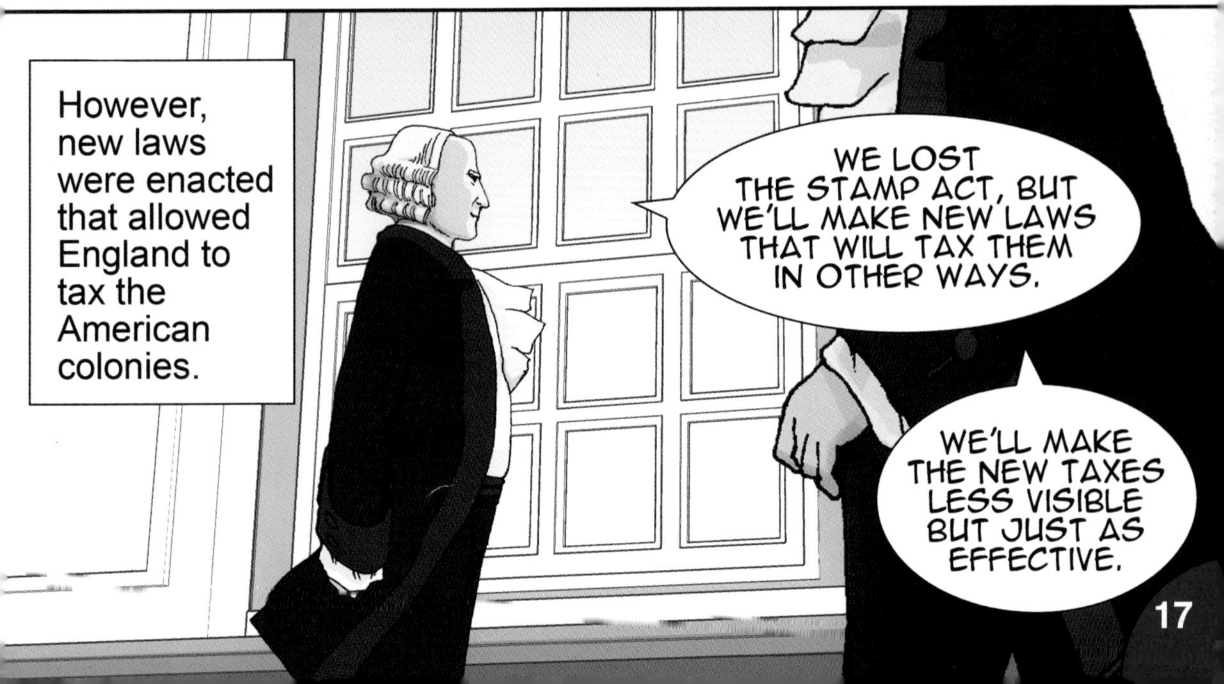
However, new laws were enacted that allowed England to tax the American colonies.
WE LOST THE STAMP ACT, BUT WE'LL MAKE NEW LAWS THAT WILL TAX THEM IN OTHER WAYS.
WE'LL MAKE THE NEW TAXES LESS VISIBLE BUT JUST AS EFFECTIVE.

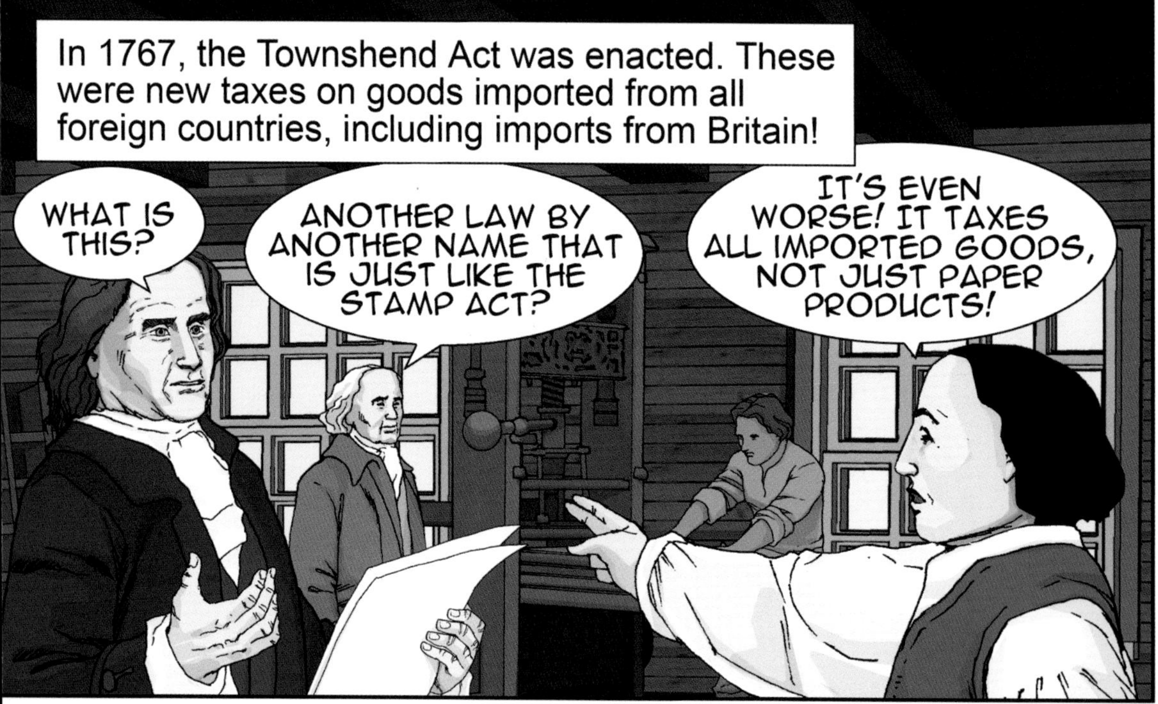
In 1767, the Townshend Act was enacted. These were new taxes on goods imported from all foreign countries, including imports from Britain!
WHAT IS THIS?
ANOTHER LAW BY ANOTHER NAME THAT IS JUST LIKE THE STAMP ACT?
IT'S EVEN WORSE! IT TAXES ALL IMPORTED GOODS, NOT JUST PAPER PRODUCTS!

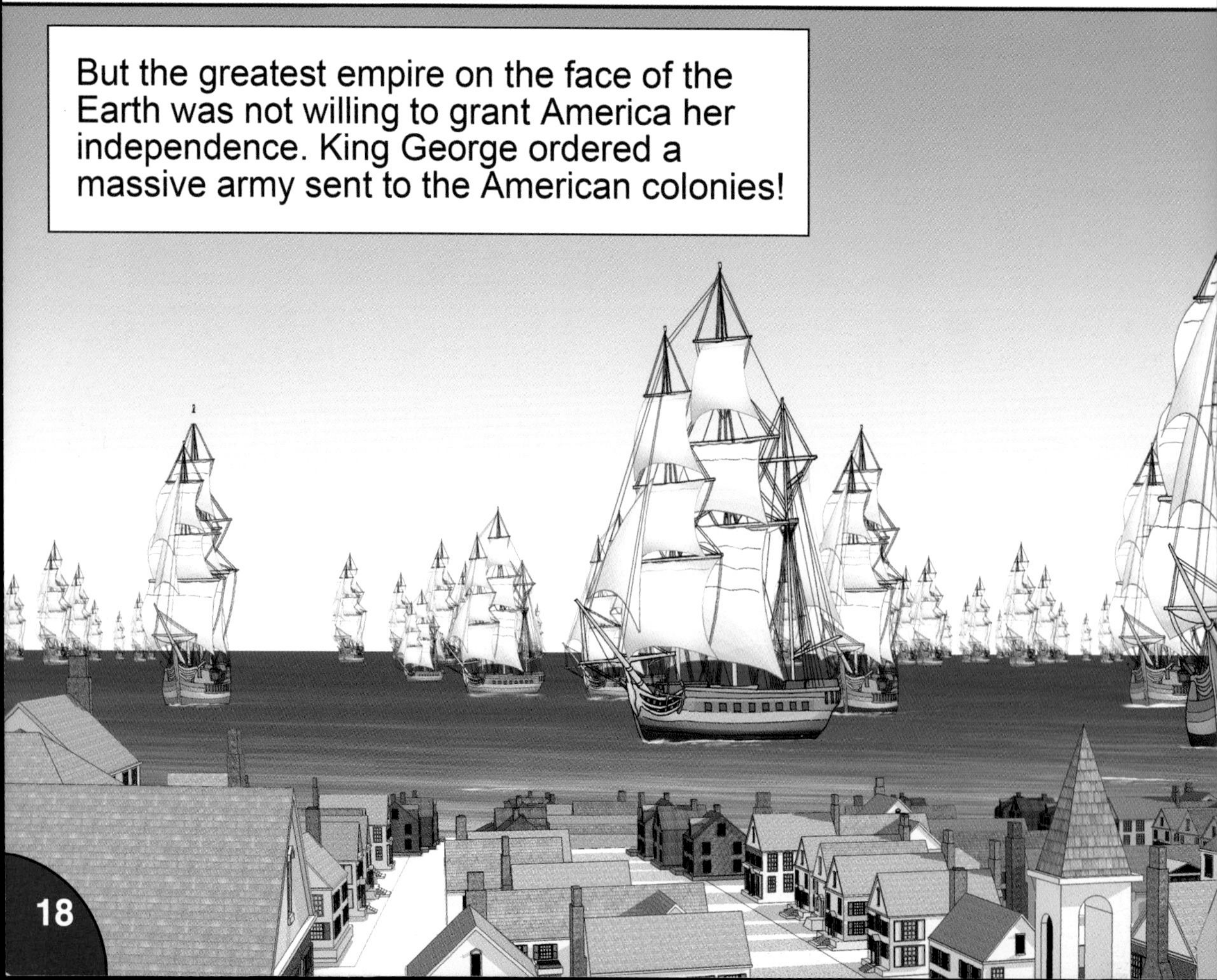
But the greatest empire on the face of the Earth was not willing to grant America her independence. King George ordered a massive army sent to the American colonies!

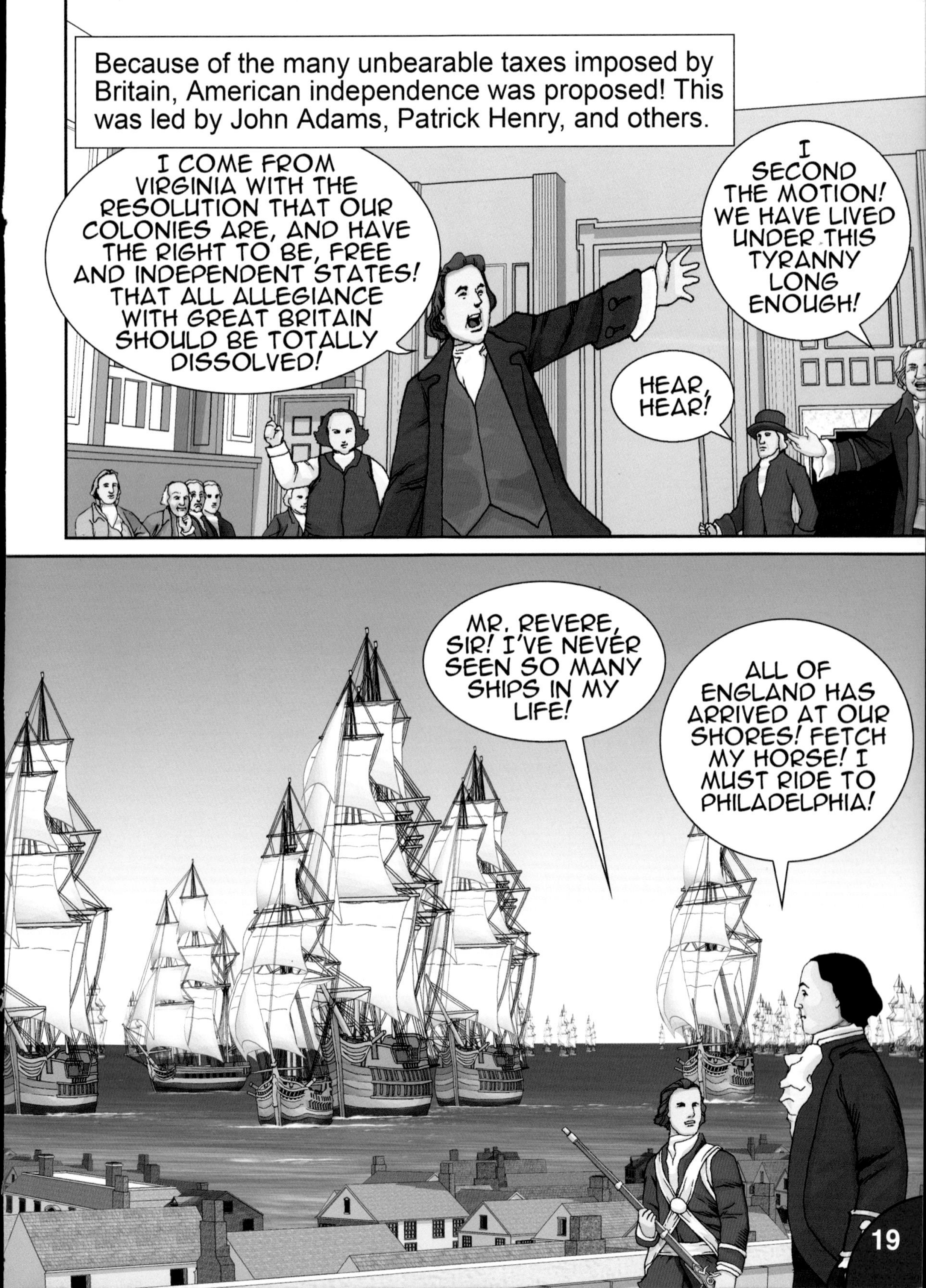
Because of the many unbearable taxes imposed by Britain, American independence was proposed! This was led by John Adams, Patrick Henry, and others.
I COME FROM VIRGINIA WITH THE RESOLUTION THAT OUR COLONIES ARE, AND HAVE THE RIGHT TO BE, FREE AND INDEPENDENT STATES! THAT ALL ALLEGIANCE WITH GREAT BRITAIN SHOULD BE TOTALLY DISSOLVED!
I SECOND THE MOTION! WE HAVE LIVED UNDER THIS TYRANNY LONG ENOUGH!
HEAR, HEAR!
MR. REVERE, SIR! I'VE NEVER SEEN SO MANY SHIPS IN MY LIFE!
ALL OF ENGLAND HAS ARRIVED AT OUR SHORES! FETCH MY HORSE! I MUST RIDE TO PHILADELPHIA!

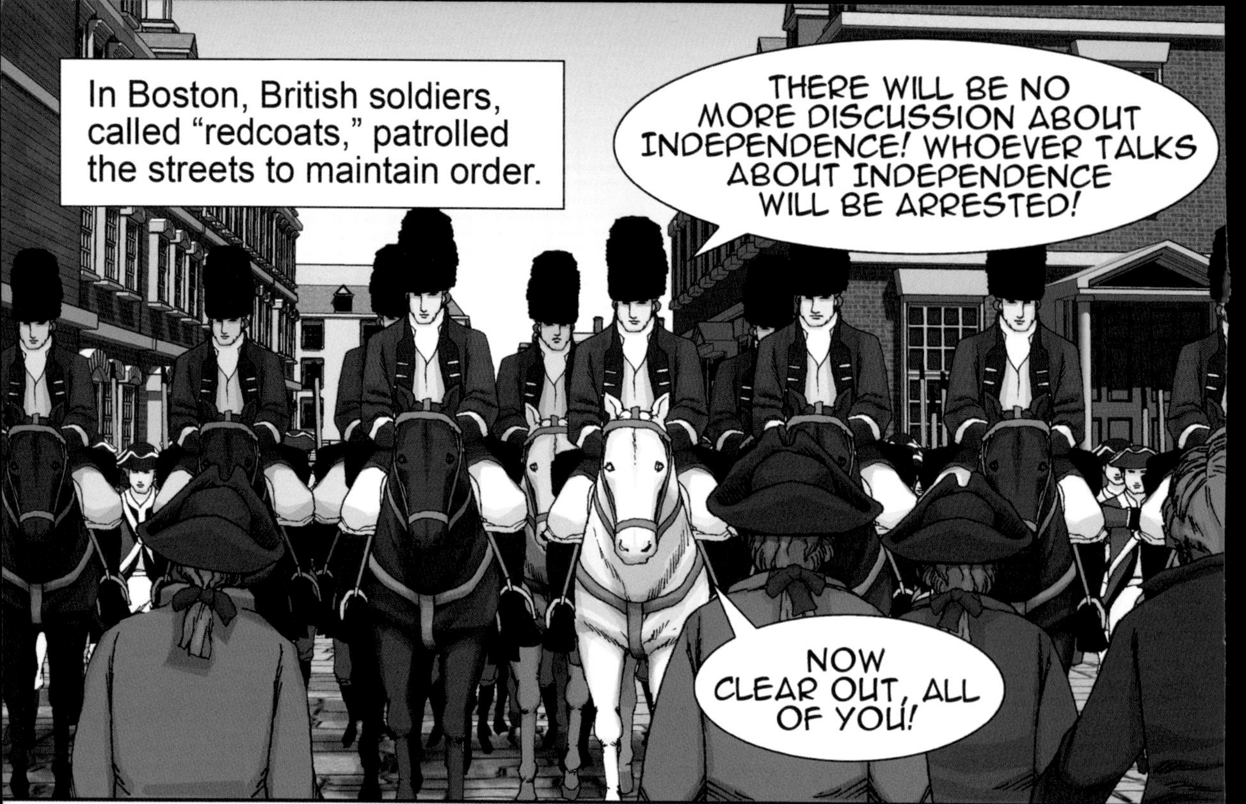
In Boston, British soldiers, called “redcoats,” patrolled the streets to maintain order.
THERE WILL BE NO MORE DISCUSSION ABOUT INDEPENDENCE! WHOEVER TALKS ABOUT INDEPENDENCE WILL BE ARRESTED!
NOW CLEAR OUT, ALL OF YOU!

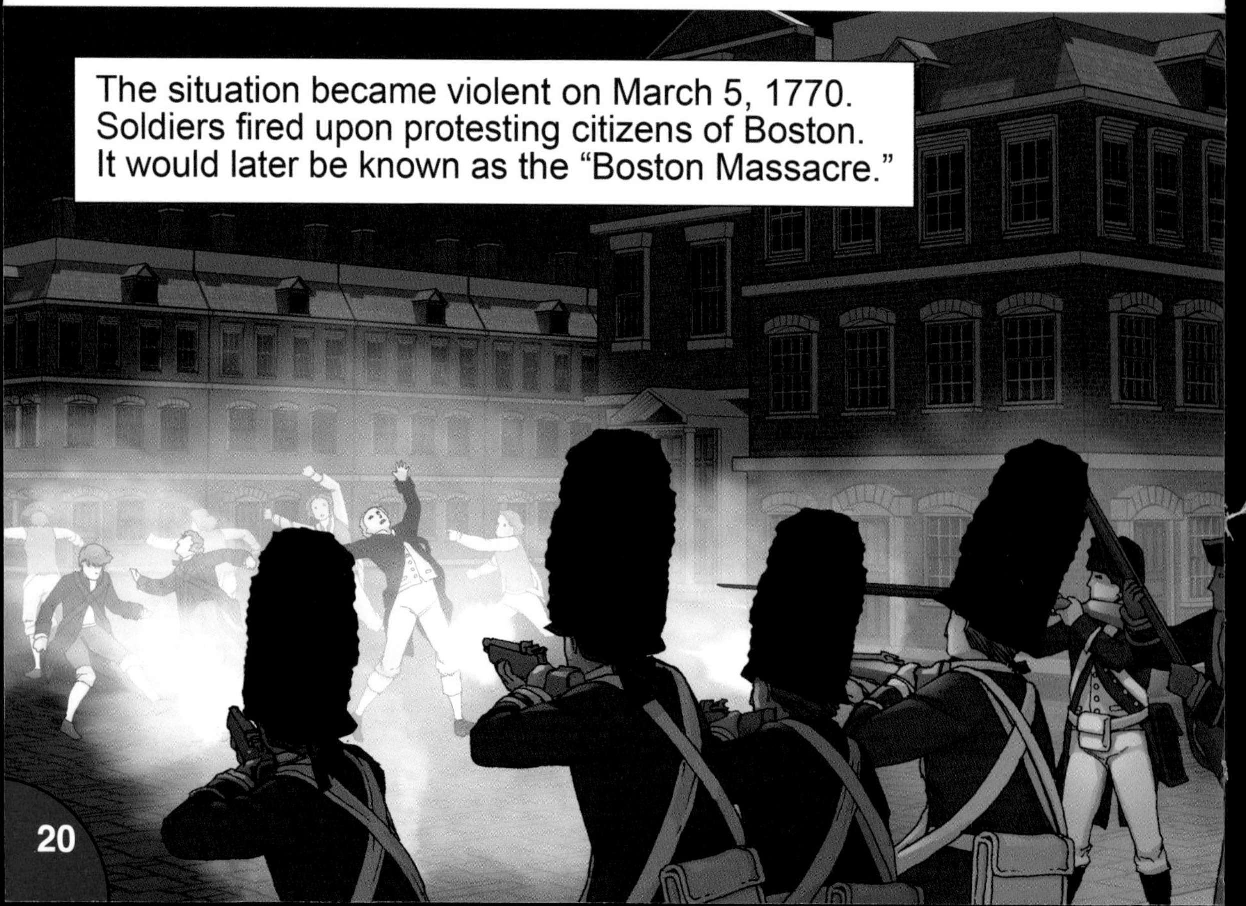
The situation became violent on March 5, 1770. Soldiers fired upon protesting citizens of Boston. It would later be known as the “Boston Massacre.”

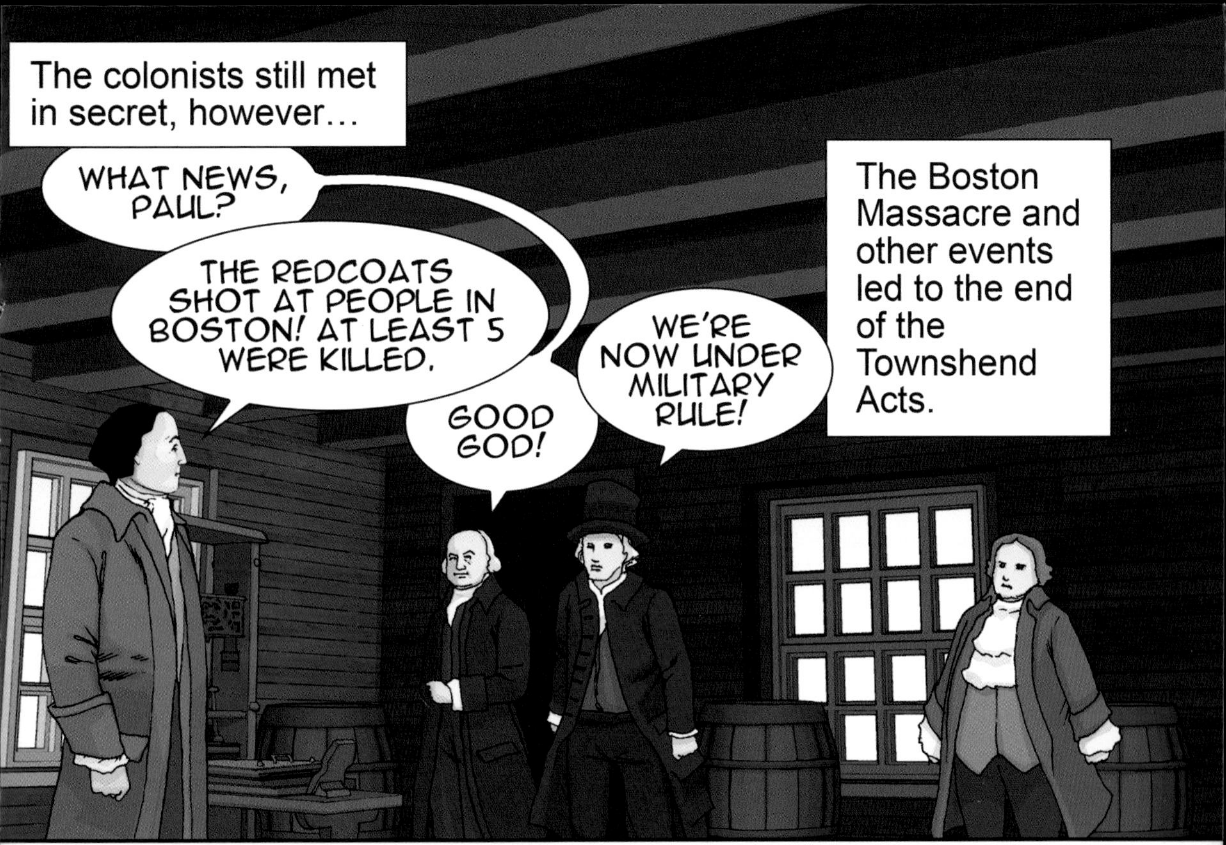
The colonists still met in secret, however…
WHAT NEWS, PAUL?
THE REDCOATS SHOT AT PEOPLE IN BOSTON! AT LEAST 5 WERE KILLED.
GOOD GOD!
WE'RE NOW UNDER MILITARY RULE!
The Boston Massacre and other events led to the end of the Townshend Acts.

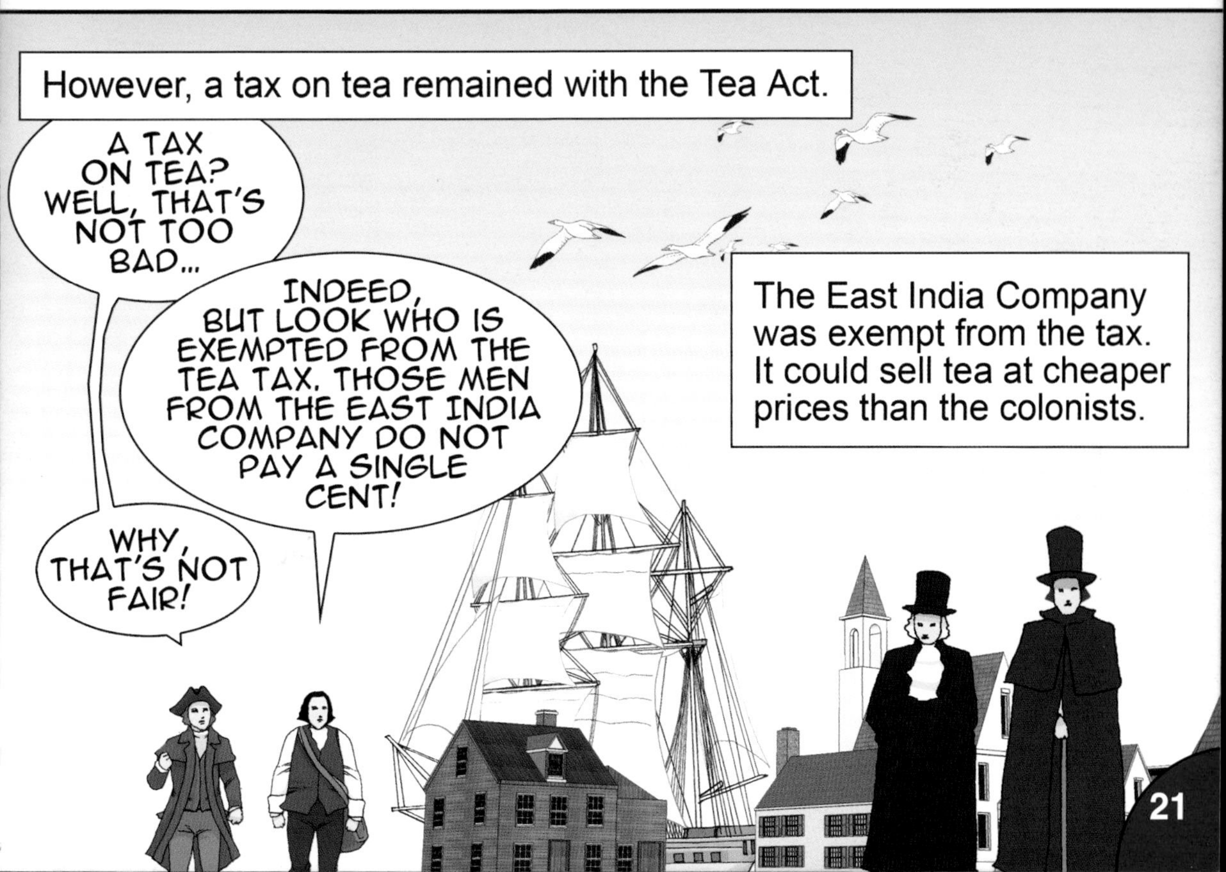
However, a tax on tea remained with the Tea Act.
A TAX ON TEA? WELL, THAT'S NOT TOO BAD...
INDEED, BUT LOOK WHO IS EXEMPTED FROM THE TEA TAX. THOSE MEN FROM THE EAST INDIA COMPANY DO NOT PAY A SINGLE CENT!
WHY, THAT'S NOT FAIR!
The East India Company was exempt from the tax. It could sell tea at cheaper prices than the colonists.

Chapter 5 The Boston Tea Party

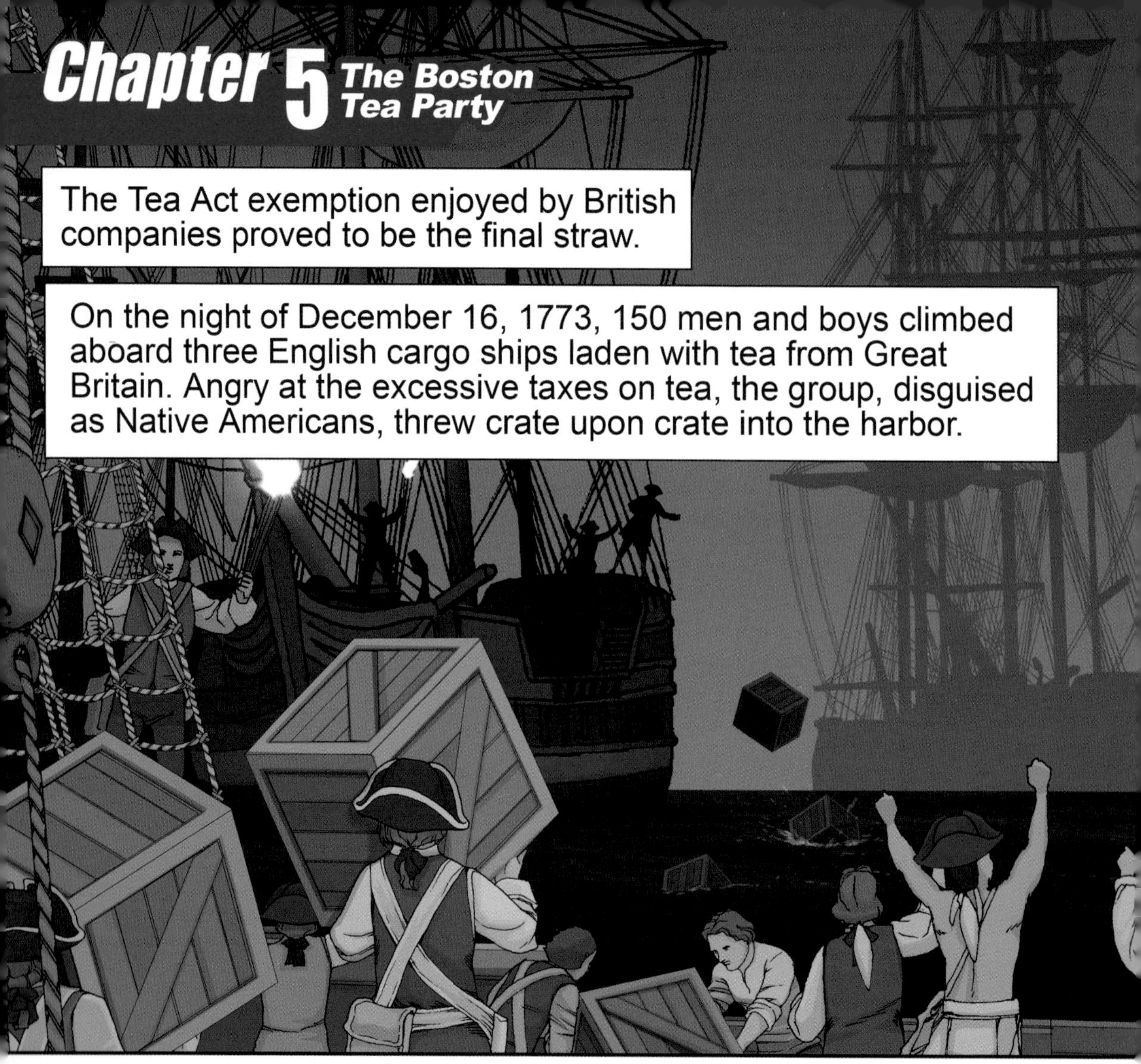
The Tea Act exemption enjoyed by British companies proved to be the final straw.
On the night of December 16, 1773, 150 men and boys climbed aboard three English cargo ships laden with tea from Great Britain. Angry at the excessive taxes on tea, the group, disguised as Native Americans, threw crate upon crate into the harbor.

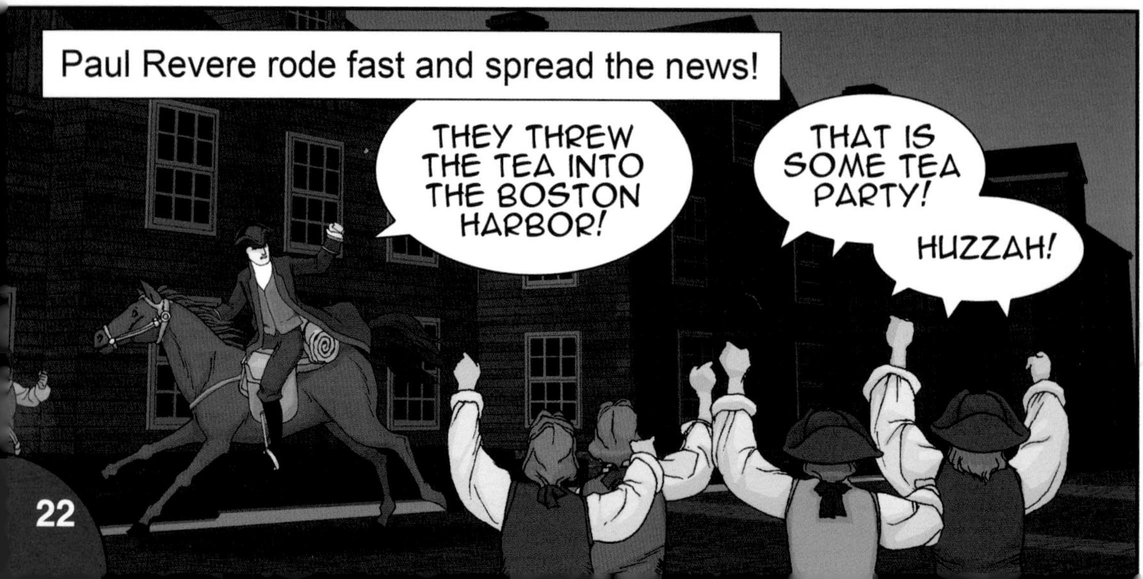
Paul Revere rode fast and spread the news!
THEY THREW THE TEA INTO THE BOSTON HARBOR!
THAT IS SOME TEA PARTY!
HUZZAH!

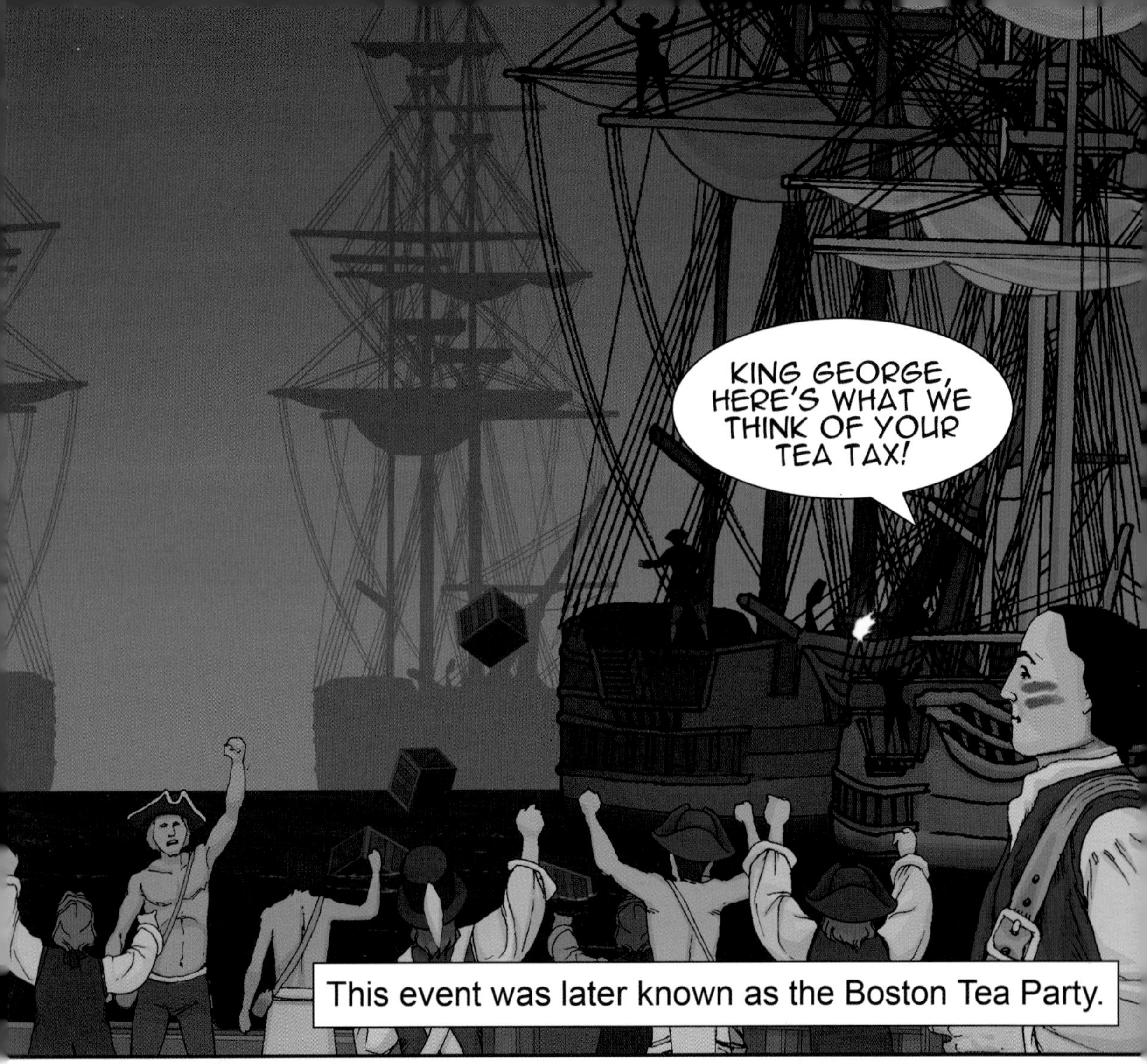
KING GEORGE, HERE'S WHAT WE THINK OF YOUR TEA TAX!
This event was later known as the Boston Tea Party.

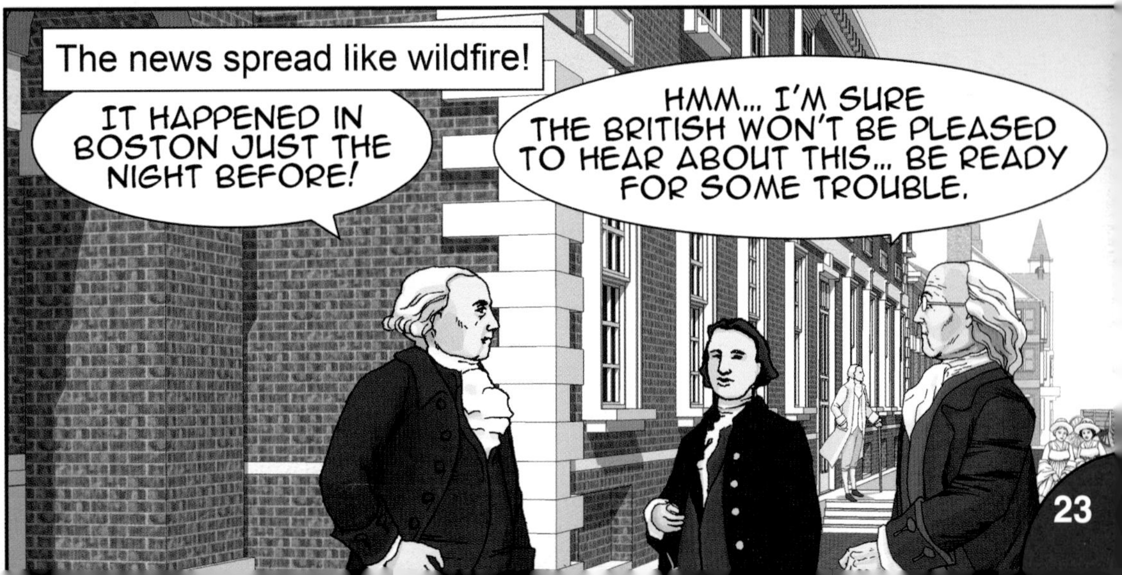
The news spread like wildfire!
IT HAPPENED IN BOSTON JUST THE NIGHT BEFORE!
HMM... I'M SURE THE BRITISH WON'T BE PLEASED TO HEAR ABOUT THIS... BE READY FOR SOME TROUBLE.

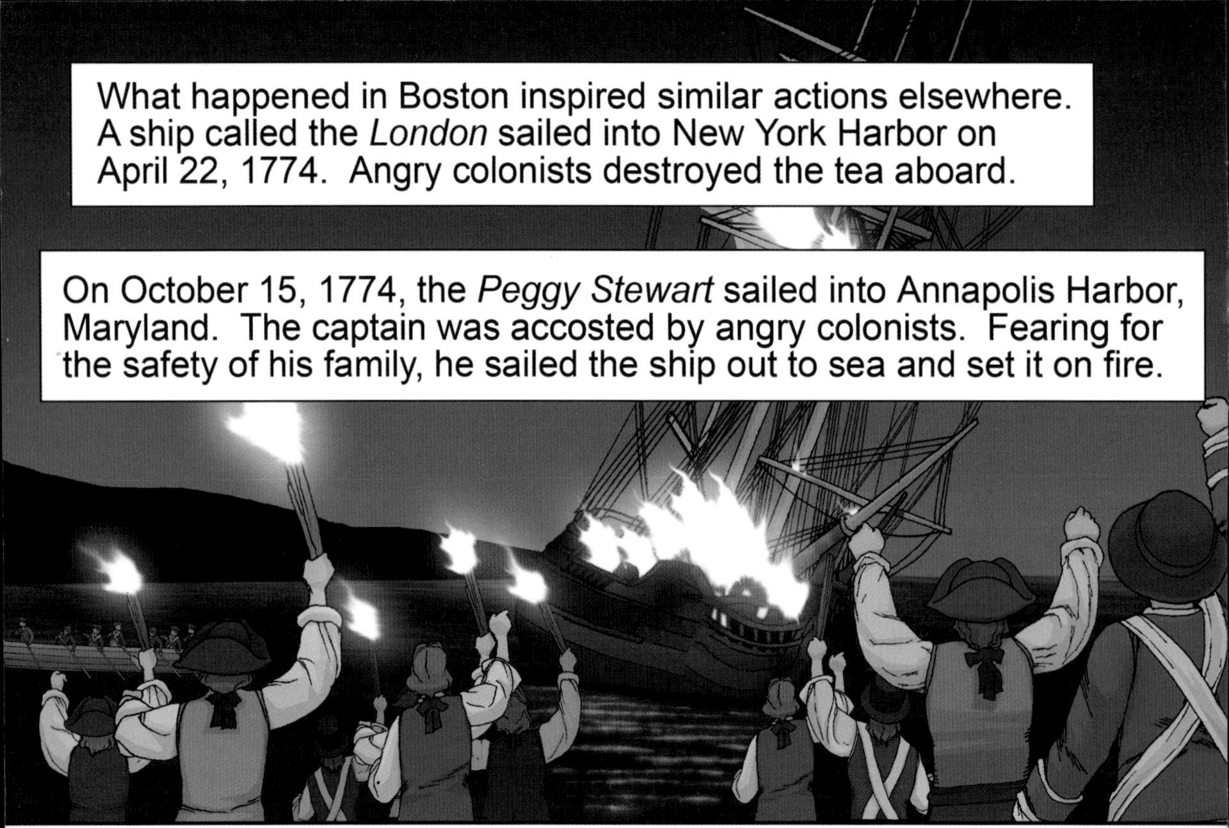
What happened in Boston inspired similar actions elsewhere. A ship called the *London* sailed into New York Harbor on April 22, 1774. Angry colonists destroyed the tea aboard.
On October 15, 1774, the *Peggy Stewart* sailed into Annapolis Harbor, Maryland. The captain was accosted by angry colonists. Fearing for the safety of his family, he sailed the ship out to sea and set it on fire.

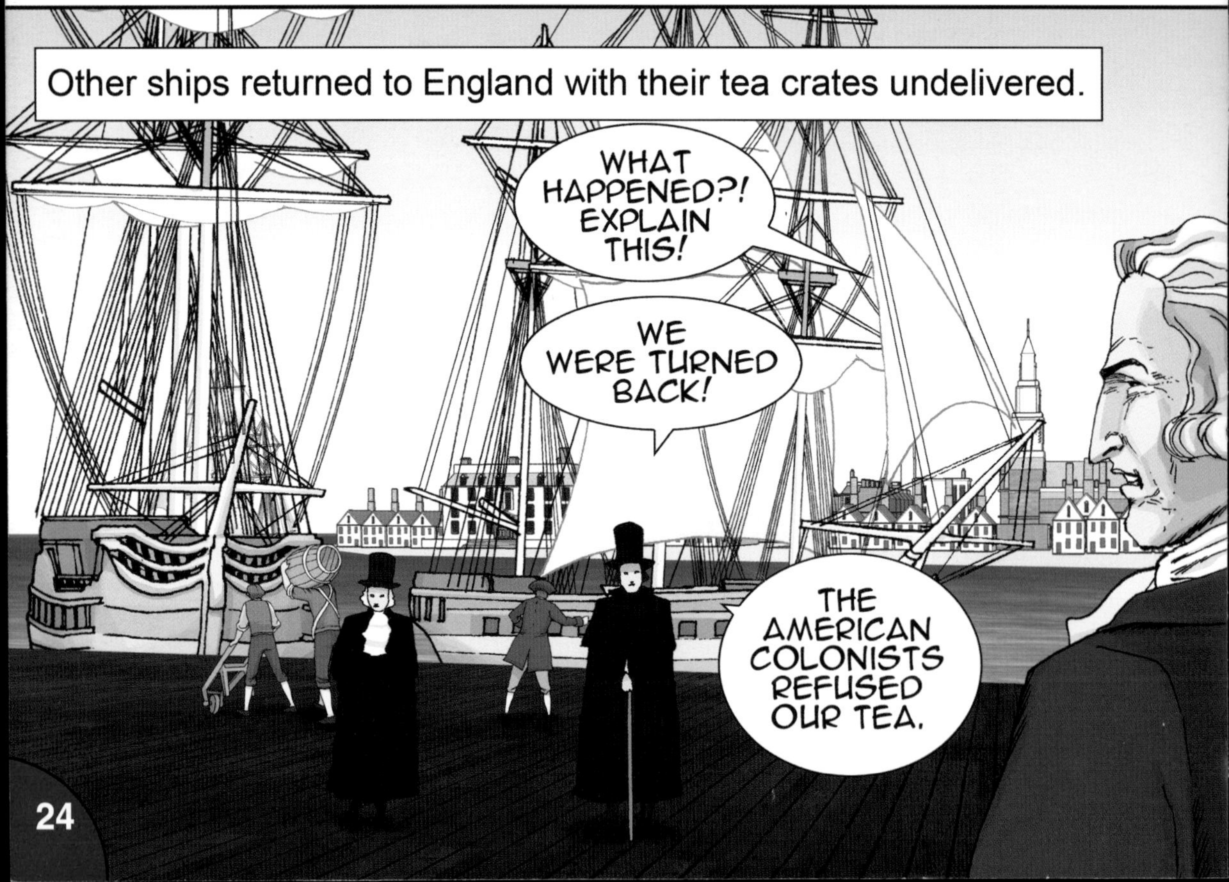
Other ships returned to England with their tea crates undelivered.
WHAT HAPPENED?! EXPLAIN THIS!
WE WERE TURNED BACK!
THE AMERICAN COLONISTS REFUSED OUR TEA.

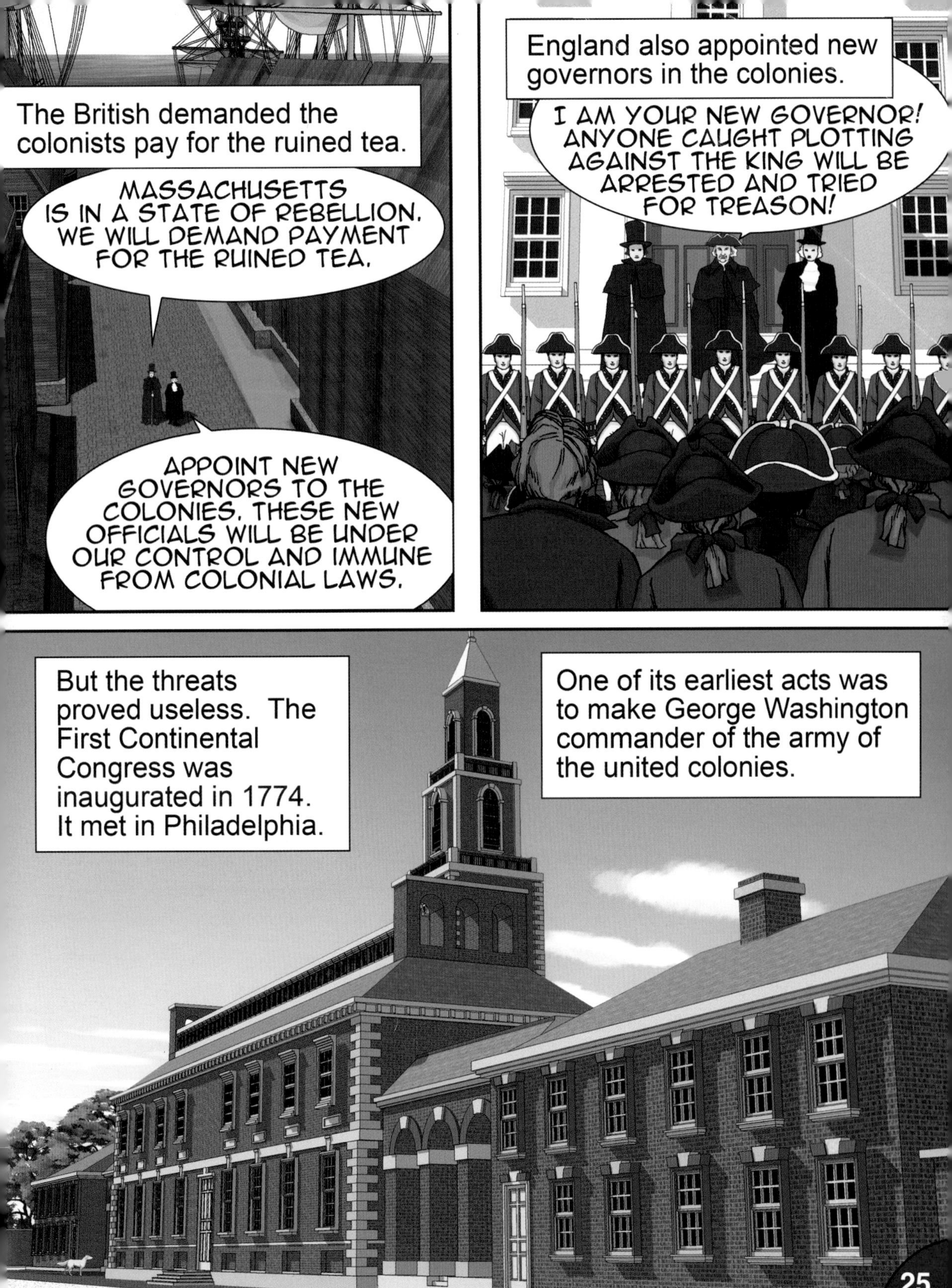
The British demanded the colonists pay for the ruined tea.
MASSACHUSETTS IS IN A STATE OF REBELLION. WE WILL DEMAND PAYMENT FOR THE RUINED TEA.
APPOINT NEW GOVERNORS TO THE COLONIES. THESE NEW OFFICIALS WILL BE UNDER OUR CONTROL AND IMMUNE FROM COLONIAL LAWS.
England also appointed new governors in the colonies.
I AM YOUR NEW GOVERNOR! ANYONE CAUGHT PLOTTING AGAINST THE KING WILL BE ARRESTED AND TRIED FOR TREASON!
But the threats proved useless. The First Continental Congress was inaugurated in 1774. It met in Philadelphia.
One of its earliest acts was to make George Washington commander of the army of the united colonies.

Chapter 6 Independence At Last!

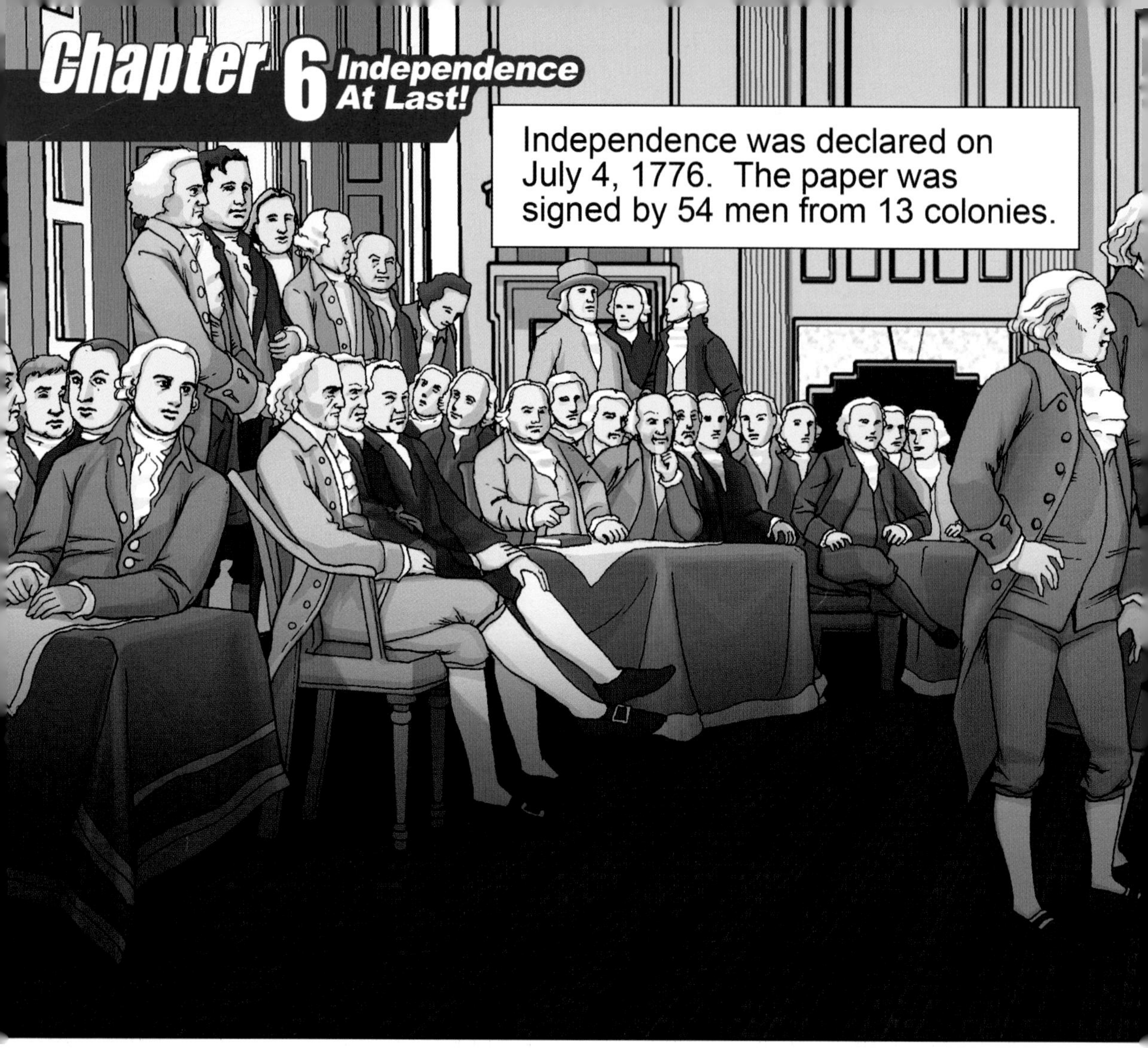
Independence was declared on July 4, 1776. The paper was signed by 54 men from 13 colonies.

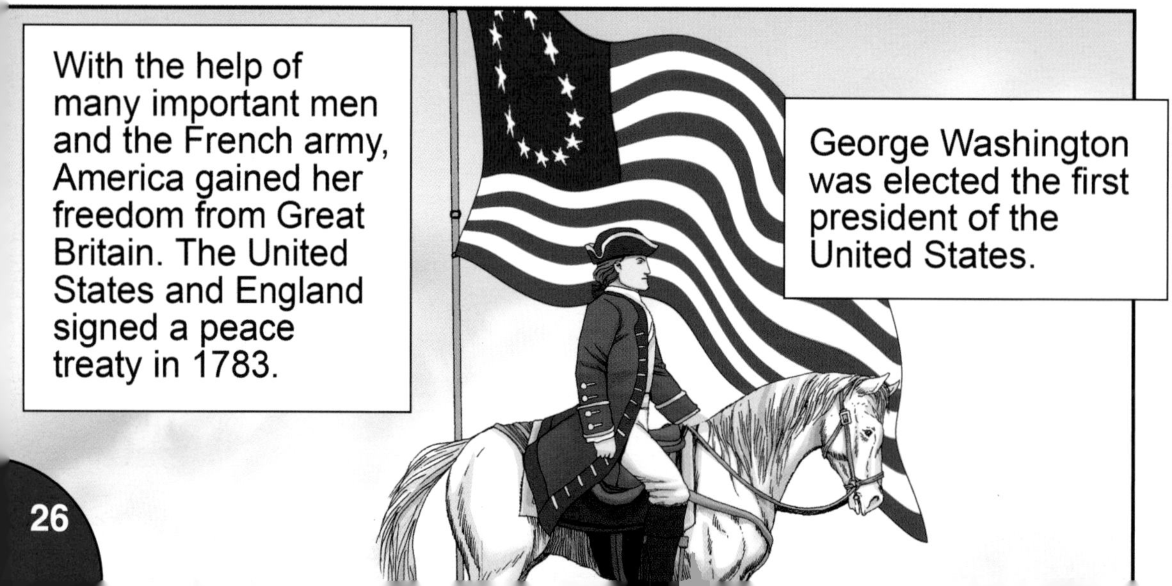
With the help of many important men and the French army, America gained her freedom from Great Britain. The United States and England signed a peace treaty in 1783.
George Washington was elected the first president of the United States.

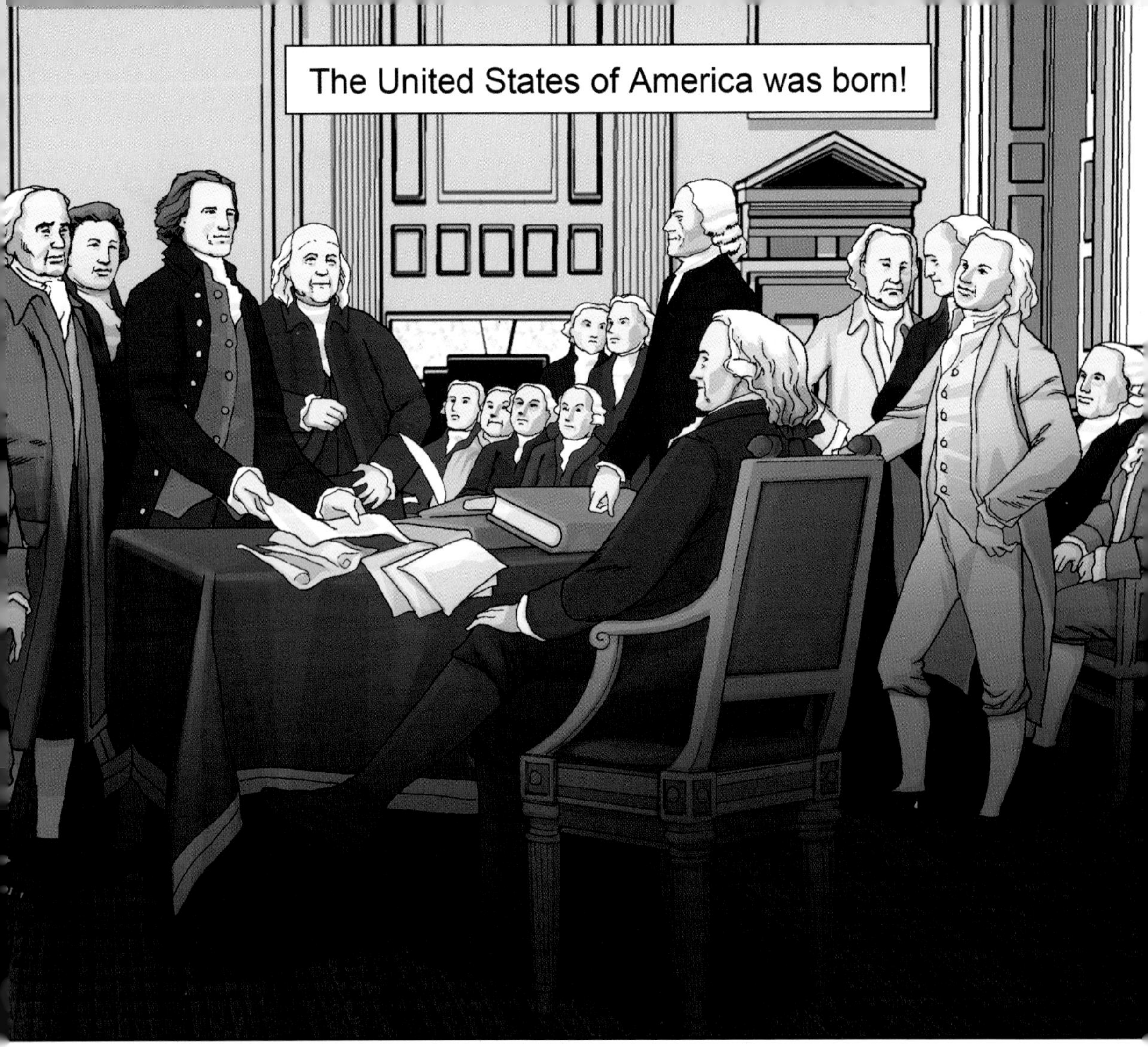
The United States of America was born!

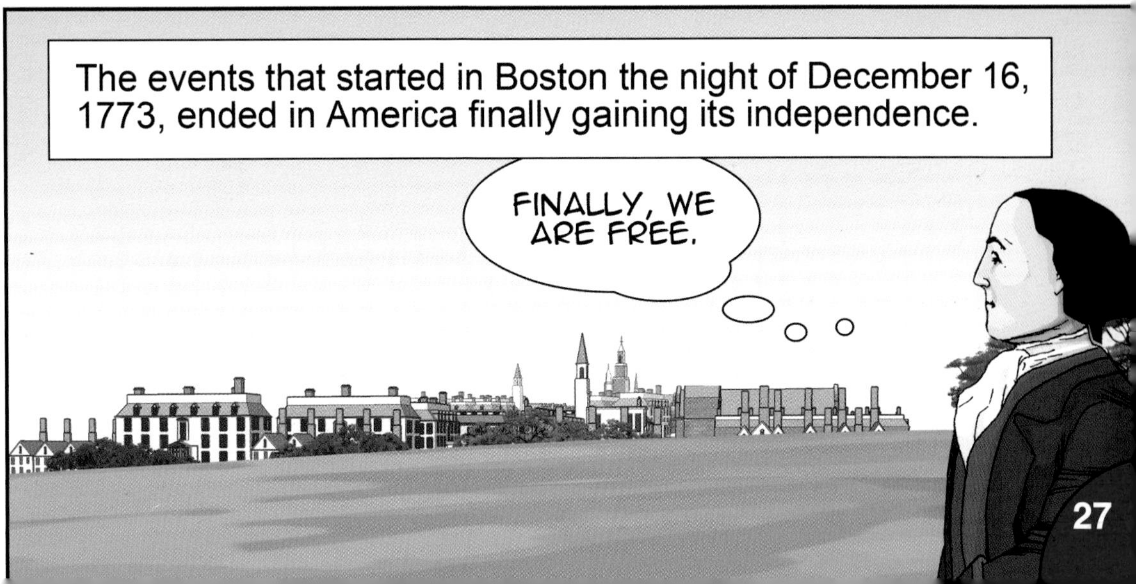
The events that started in Boston the night of December 16, 1773, ended in America finally gaining its independence.
FINALLY, WE ARE FREE.

Timeline

1600s - The East India Trade Company was established.

1754 - The French and Indian War began.

1764 to 1767 - A series of taxes, including the Sugar Act, Stamp Act and Townshend Act, were implemented to help pay for the war and to keep a standing army in the colonies.

March 5, 1770 - The Boston Massacre occurred.

May 10, 1773 - The Tea Act was passed to save the East India Trade Company from bankruptcy.

November 27, 1773 - Three ships under the protection of the Tea Act arrived in Boston.

December 1773 - Samuel Adams and the Sons of Liberty prevented the ships from being unloaded but would not prevent the tax from being paid.

December 16, 1773 - About 60 men dressed as Mohawk Indians boarded three British ships and dumped the tea overboard.

1774 - Similar tea parties occurred in New York and Annapolis.

March 1774 - The Intolerable Acts were passed, closing Boston Harbor.

April 19, 1775 - The battles at Lexington and Concord started the American Revolution.

THE AMERICAN COLONIES - 1775

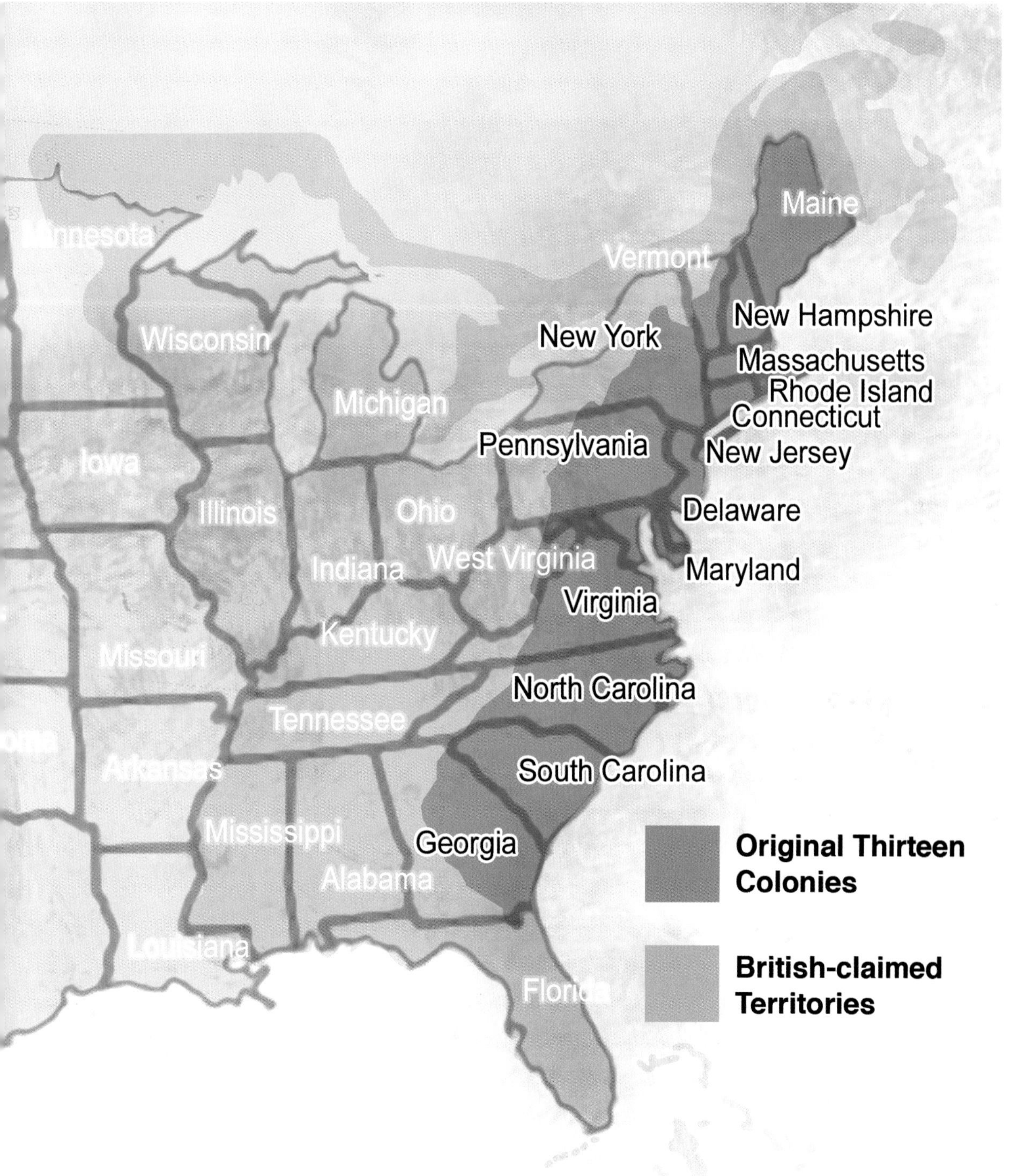
Maine
Vermont
New Hampshire
New York
Massachusetts
Rhode Island
Connecticut
Pennsylvania
New Jersey
Delaware
Maryland
Virginia
North Carolina
South Carolina
Georgia
Minnesota
Wisconsin
Michigan
Iowa
Illinois
Ohio
Indiana
West Virginia
Kentucky
Missouri
Tennessee
Arkansas
Mississippi
Alabama
Louisiana
Florida
Original Thirteen Colonies
British-claimed Territories

In Congress, July 4, 1776.

The unanimous Declaration of the thirteen united States of America.

When, in the course of human events, it becomes necessary for one people to dissolve the political bonds which have connected them with another, and to assume among the powers of the earth, the separate and equal station to which the laws of nature and of nature's God entitle them, a decent respect to the opinions of mankind requires that they should declare the causes which impel them to the separation.

We hold these truths to be self-evident, that all men are created equal, that they are endowed by their Creator with certain unalienable rights, that among these are life, liberty and the pursuit of happiness. That to secure these rights, governments are instituted among men, deriving their just powers from the consent of the governed. That whenever any form of government becomes destructive to these ends, it is the right of the people to alter or to abolish it, and to institute new government, laying its foundation on such principles and organizing its powers in such form, as to them shall seem most likely to effect their safety and happiness. Prudence, indeed, will dictate that governments long established should not be changed for light and transient causes; and accordingly all experience hath shown that mankind are more disposed to suffer, while evils are sufferable, than to right themselves by abolishing the forms to which they are accustomed. But when a long train of abuses and usurpations, pursuing invariably the same object evinces a design to reduce them under absolute despotism, it is their right, it is their duty, to throw off such government, and to provide new guards for their future security. --Such has been the patient sufferance of these colonies; and such is now the necessity which constrains them to alter their former systems of government. The history of the present King of Great Britain is a history of repeated injuries and usurpations, all having in direct object the establishment of an absolute tyranny over these states. To prove this, let facts be submitted to a candid world.

He has refused his assent to laws, the most wholesome and necessary for the public good. He has forbidden his governors to pass laws of immediate and pressing importance, unless suspended in their operation till his assent should be obtained; and when so suspended, he has utterly neglected to attend to them. He has refused to pass other laws for the accommodation of large districts of people, unless those people would relinquish the right of representation in the legislature, a right inestimable to them and formidable to tyrants only. He has called together legislative bodies at places unusual, uncomfortable, and distant from the depository of their public records, for the sole purpose of fatiguing them into compliance with his measures. He has dissolved representative houses repeatedly, for opposing with manly firmness his invasions on the rights of the people. He has refused for a long time, after such dissolutions, to cause others to be elected; whereby the legislative powers, incapable of annihilation, have returned to the people at large for their exercise; the state remaining in the meantime exposed to all the dangers of invasion from without, and convulsions within. He has endeavored to prevent the population of these states; for that purpose obstructing the laws for naturalization of foreigners; refusing to pass others to encourage their migration hither, and raising the conditions of new appropriations of lands. He has obstructed the administration of justice, by refusing his assent to laws for establishing judiciary powers. He has made judges dependent on his will alone, for the tenure of their offices, and the amount and payment of their salaries. He has erected a multitude of new offices, and sent hither swarms of officers to harass our people, and eat out their substance. He has kept among us, in times of peace, standing armies without the consent of our legislature.
He has affected to render the military independent of and superior to civil power. He has combined with others to subject us to a jurisdiction foreign to our constitution, and unacknowledged by our laws; giving his assent to their acts of pretended legislation: For quartering large bodies of armed troops among us: For protecting them, by mock trial, from punishment for any murders which they should commit on the inhabitants of these states: For cutting off our trade with all parts of the world: For imposing taxes on us without our consent: For depriving us in many cases, of the benefits of trial by jury:
For transporting us beyond seas to be tried for pretended offenses: For abolishing the free system of English laws in a neighboring province, establishing therein an arbitrary government, and enlarging its boundaries so as to render it at once an example and fit instrument for introducing the same absolute rule in these colonies: For taking away our charters, abolishing our most valuable laws, and altering fundamentally the forms of our governments: For suspending our own legislatures, and declaring themselves invested with power to legislate for us in all cases whatsoever. He has abdicated government here, by declaring us out of his protection and waging war against us. He has plundered our seas, ravaged our coasts, burned our towns, and destroyed the lives of our people. He is at this time transporting large armies of foreign mercenaries to complete the works of death, desolation and tyranny, already begun with circumstances of cruelty and perfidy scarcely paralleled in the most barbarous ages, and totally unworthy the head of a civilized nation. He has constrained our fellow citizens taken captive on the high seas to bear arms against their country, to become the executioners of their friends and brethren, or to fall themselves by their hands. He has excited domestic insurrections amongst us, and has endeavored to bring on the inhabitants of our frontiers, the merciless Indian savages, whose known rule of warfare, is undistinguished destruction of all ages, sexes and conditions. In every stage of these oppressions we have petitioned for redress in the most humble terms: our repeated petitions have been answered only by repeated injury. A prince, whose character is thus marked by every act which may define a tyrant, is unfit to be the ruler of a free people. Nor have we been wanting in attention to our British brethren. We have warned them from time to time of attempts by their legislature to extend an unwarrantable jurisdiction over us. We have reminded them of the circumstances of our emigration and settlement here. We have appealed to their native justice and magnanimity, and we have conjured them by the ties of our common kindred to disavow these usurpations, which, would inevitably interrupt our connections and correspondence. We must, therefore, acquiesce in the necessity, which denounces our separation, and hold them, as we hold the rest of mankind, enemies in war, in peace friends.

We, therefore, the representatives of the United States of America, in General Congress, assembled, appealing to the Supreme Judge of the world for the rectitude of our intentions, do, in the name, and by the authority of the good people of these colonies, solemnly publish and declare, that these united colonies are, and of right ought to be free and independent states; that they are absolved from all allegiance to the British Crown, and that all political connection between them and the state of Great Britain, is and ought to be totally dissolved; and that as free and independent states, they have full power to levy war, conclude peace, contract alliances, establish commerce, and to do all other acts and things which independent states may of right do. And for the support of this declaration, with a firm reliance on the protection of Divine Providence, we mutually pledge to each other our lives, our fortunes and our sacred honor.

Button Gwinnett
Lyman Hall
Geo Walton.

Wm Hooper
Joseph Hewes,
John Penn

Edward Rutledge.

Thos Heyward Junr.
Thomas Lynch Junr.
Arthur Middleton

John Hancock

Samuel Chase
Wm Paca
Thos Stone
Charles Carroll of Carrollton

George Wythe
Richard Henry Lee
Th Jefferson
Benja Harrison
Thos Nelson jr.
Francis Lightfoot Lee
Carter Braxton

Robt Morris
Benjamin Rush
Benja Franklin
John Morton
Geo Clymer
Jas Smith.
Geo Taylor
James Wilson
Geo. Ross
Caesar Rodney
Geo Read
Tho McKean

Wm Floyd
Phil. Livingston
Frans Lewis
Lewis Morris

Richd Stockton
Jno Witherspoon
Fras Hopkinson
John Hart
Abra Clark

Josiah Bartlett
Wm Whipple
Saml Adams
John Adams
Robt Treat Paine
Elbridge Gerry
Step Hopkins
William Ellery
Roger Sherman
Saml Huntington
Wm Williams
Oliver Wolcott
Matthew Thornton

Glossary

accost - to approach in an angry or hostile manner.

excessive - an amount or degree too great to be reasonable or acceptable.

exempt - released from a rule or law that others must follow.

inaugurate - to swear into a political office.

military rule - law administered by the military of the ruling government.

tactic - a method or a device used to achieve a goal.

tyranny - a government where one person has absolute power. The person in power is called a tyrant.

Web Sites

To learn more about the Boston Tea Party, visit ABDO Publishing Company on the World Wide Web at **www.abdopublishing.com.** Web sites about the Boston Tea Party are featured on our Book Links page. These links are routinely monitored and updated to provide the most current information available.

Index